◆ CHILDREN'S ◆
DRESSING UP
IDEAS TO MAKE IN A DAY

DESIGNS BY GLORIA WITTKE

WINDWARD

House Editor: Dorothea Hall
Editor: Joy Mayhew
Costume Designs: Gloria Wittke
Art Editor: Caroline Dewing
Designer: Caroline Hill
Production: Richard Churchill

Published by Windward, an imprint owned by
W. H. Smith & Son Limited Registered No. 237811. England
Trading as WHS Distributors, St. John's House,
East Street, Leicester LE1 6NE

© Marshall Cavendish Limited 1987

ISBN 0 7112 0464 0

Typeset by Bookworm Typesetting, Manchester, England
Printed and bound by L.E.G.O., Italy

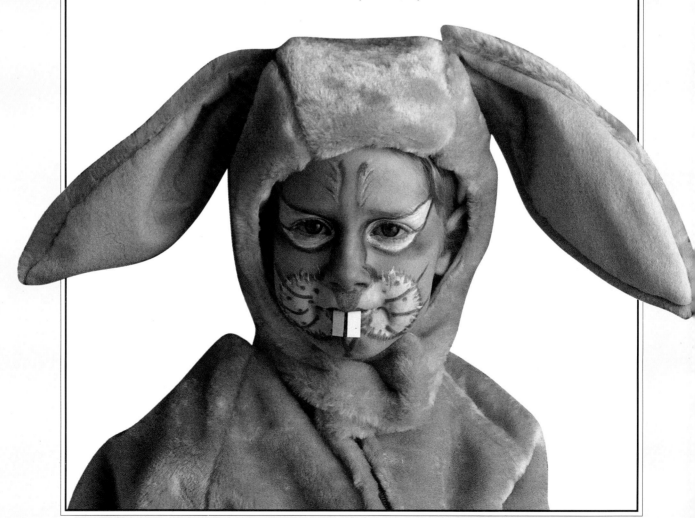

Contents

Introduction 8

Before you Begin 9

Clowning Around 10

High Wire Act 16

Rodeo Show 20

Roll up, Roll up 26

Fairytale 32

Gone Fishing 38

Sinbad the Sailor 44

Little Princess 48

Good Knight 54

Jungle Cat 60

Big Fat Hen 66

Funny Bunny 72

Stitch a Witch 76

Space Invader 82

Out for the Count 88

Suppliers 93

Introduction

In recent years fancy dress parties have become increasingly popular with younger children, who generally adore dressing up and require very little by way of encouragement. Here in Dressing Up you'll find a fantastic collection of fancy dress ideas you can make for children between the ages of six to nine. There are colourful outfits for all occasions from jolly circus characters and delightful flower fairies to wicked-looking witches and space invaders.

The designer, Gloria Wittke, has made the costumes as simple as possible, to be within the scope of the average home dressmaker. Finishing is kept to a minimum – on non-fraying fabrics, for example, raw edges are left unfinished, and where possible, hems and turnings are stuck in place, for simplicity and speed. She has introduced lots of original design features that help to give these costumes their touch of brilliance. There's the flower fairy's coronet made from delicate gauze flower petals, and her matching wand, the witch's evil-looking green snake and the rabbit's large, juicy carrot – all examples of Gloria's inventiveness.

To complete the effect, Ozzie Alam has specially created the face make-up. Her witty designs complement each fancy dress costume, adding a colourful, finishing touch with real theatrical flair.

With this superb collection of 15 original costumes complete with graph patterns and easy-to-follow instructions, you'll find dressing up your children most exciting – creating costumes the children will love to wear.

Before you Begin

How to enlarge a graph pattern

The patterns for the costumes given in the following pages are drawn on a squared grid based on metric measurements where each square represents five centimetres.

To scale up the pattern, you should use graph paper that has squares of a corresponding size. You can either buy dressmaker's pattern paper, or mark sheets of plain paper into 5cm squares.

In addition to paper, you will need both ordinary and coloured pencils, long and short metric rulers, a set-square (if ruling your own paper), paper-cutting scissors and adhesive tape for joining together sheets of paper.

The graph patterns are given in one size only, to fit six to nine year olds. Each costume is designed with plenty of ease, so that the length may be the only area that requires adjusting to the individual child.

The paper pattern

1 Make sure that the sheets of paper are sufficiently large to take the pattern of your choice by counting and comparing the squares. If not, then join suitable pieces together. When using plain paper, check the outer edges with a set-square, to see if they are square. Trim, if necessary. Using a long ruler, and pencil, mark the edges of the paper both ways, at 5cm intervals. Rule the paper into squares.

2 Using a coloured pencil, and counting and comparing the squares, copy the graph pattern onto the larger squares of your paper. Mark the points where the outline of the pattern crosses the grid lines, then join up these marks to complete the shape. Repeat for the remaining pattern pieces.

3 Using a contrasting colour, rule in the arrows (straight grain of fabric) then mark in all notches, dots, dashes, the names of the pattern pieces and all other useful information. Cut out the pattern.

Face make-up

When applying make-up to the face it is important to keep the hair well away from the face area. Tuck the hair inside a hairnet or stretch a wide hairband (or bandage) firmly around the head, just above the hairline.

For applying the make-up you will need a selection of small make-up sponges, soft applicators and blusher brushes, plus cleansing cream and paper tissues (or cotton wool balls) for finally removing it.

9

Clowning Around

Who will be able to resist playing the clown in this sensational outfit? Vast, baggy pants and a giant bow tie are complemented by a crazy scarlet wig. All you need to complete the outfit are a red T-shirt, tights and outsized shiny shoes – plus the obligatory zany face make-up!

You will need
For an outfit to fit ages 6-9 (trouser length, 65cm from waist, adjustable by braces)

1.70m of 115cm-wide spot-printed yellow satin
50cm by 60cm of diamond-printed yellow satin
1.20m of 2.5cm-wide nylon boning
30cm of 90cm-wide heavy-weight bonded interfacing
30cm by 50cm of lightweight bonded interfacing
Eight large red buttons (about 6cm in diameter)
40cm of 2.5cm-wide black elastic
1.50m of 4cm-wide yellow grosgrain ribbon
Buckram hat mould (or cap-shaped hat crown)
100g of bright red chunky knitting yarn
One large press stud
Dressmaker's pattern paper
Matching sewing threads

Make-up
White foundation cream
White face powder
Red lipstick
Black kohl pencil

Accessories
Red T-shirt
White gloves (larger than child's hand)
Red socks or tights
Red patent leather shoes (several sizes larger than foot)
Yellow satin ribbon for 'laces'

Preparing the pattern
Using dressmaker's pattern paper, scale up the pattern for the trousers given on page 12. Seam allowances of 1.5cm are included on all pieces except the tab, which has 1cm seams, and the trouser legs which have a 7cm hem allowance.

Mark notches, circles, fold lines and straight-grain lines onto the pattern pieces, plus any other instructions shown on the graph, and cut out, remembering to use all-purpose scissors.

Cutting out
For the trousers, fold the spotted satin fabric right sides together with the selvedges level at the sides. Pin the pattern pieces in place following the cutting layout, making sure the arrows follow the straight grain of fabric, and cut out using sharp, dressmaker's shears. Cut out four tab pieces from lightweight interfacing.

For the bow, cut out a 30cm by 60cm rectangle of diamond-print fabric plus a 12cm square for the knot. Cut out similar pieces in heavy-weight interfacing and place on one side.

Sewing instructions
1 Trousers
With right sides together, stitch centre front and centre back seams; reinforce crotch area with a second row of stitching, about 2mm inside the first stitching line. Clip around curves and press seams open. Join front to back at sides and around inside leg; press seams open.

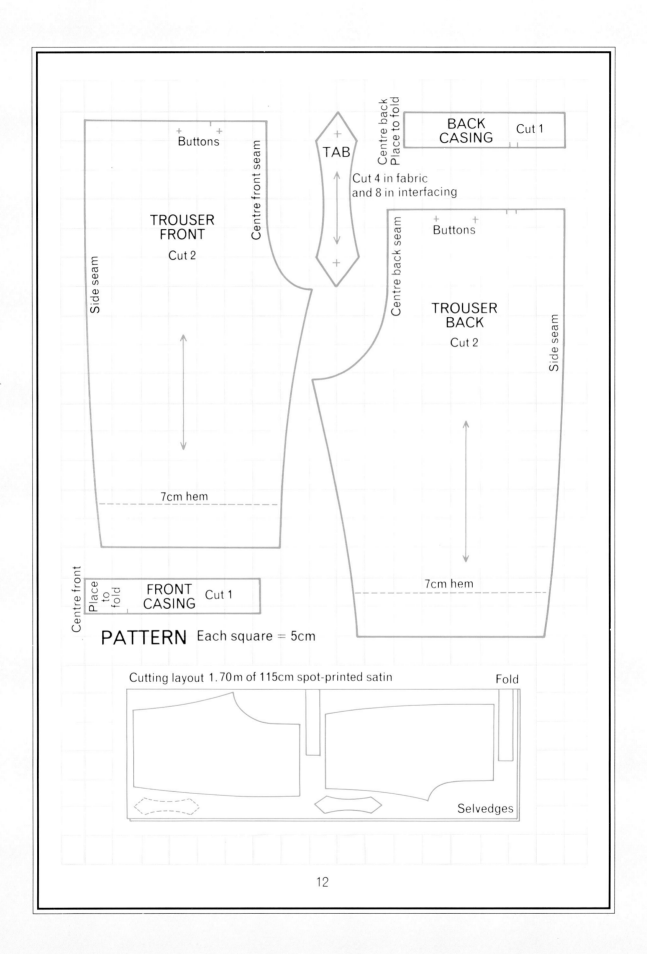

Buttons

Centre front seam

TAB

Cut 4 in fabric
and 8 in interfacing

Centre back
Place to fold

BACK
CASING   Cut 1

TROUSER
FRONT

Cut 2

Side seam

Centre back seam

Buttons

TROUSER
BACK

Cut 2

Side seam

7cm hem

7cm hem

Centre front

Place to fold

FRONT
CASING   Cut 1

PATTERN   Each square = 5cm

Cutting layout 1.70m of 115cm spot-printed satin

Fold

Selvedges

Make turnings on lower edges of legs first folding over 2cm then 5cm. Tack in place: leave until braces are adjusted for length.

Open out and join side seams of casing pieces to form a circle. Press seams open then press under 6mm around one edge of casing. With right sides together, matching notches and side seams, stitch unpressed edge of casing to upper edge of trousers. Turn folded edge over to inside so that it meets previous seam line and press. To form the casing, stitch along lower fold, leaving an opening in the stitching for the stiffening. Insert the stiffening into the casing, overlap ends by 1cm and stitch together. Slipstitch opening closed.

Note: For a less exaggerated look, shorten the length of the stiffening, if preferred.

2 Tabs and braces

Tack lightweight interfacing to wrong side of four tab pieces. With right sides together, stitch a plain fabric section to each one, leaving a small gap for turning through. Layer seams and trim corners, turn through and press. Slipstitch openings closed. Fold each tab in half lengthways and slipstitch edges of centre together (about 4cm) to form a firm loop around which the braces will be stitched. Matching circles, pin ends of tabs to outside waist edge of trousers. Sew on buttons through all thicknesses to secure tabs.

Cut the ribbon into two equal lengths for braces and neaten one raw end of each length. Attach these ends by passing them under the tab loops and machining the neatened ends down to remaining ribbon.

Cross the ribbon at the back (pin and mark the crossing point), then pass other ends through tabs at back, and tack. Try on trousers and adjust length of braces if necessary. These wide baggy trousers are meant to be worn high above the natural waistline, but should be adjusted to your liking. Trim, neaten and stitch braces as for the front. Stitch the crossing point and press on the wrong side.

Slipstitch hems at lower edge of trousers. Press to finish.

3 Bow-tie

Tack interfacing to wrong side of bow and knot pieces. With right sides together fold bow section lengthways in half and stitch long edges together, leaving ends open.

Remove the tacking stitches. Turn to right side and press. Bring raw edges together and stitch seam; press open, turn seam to inside and pin down at centre of bow. Using strong thread in the needle, make a line of running stitches through all layers along centre seam. Draw up the thread tightly and fasten off firmly.

Fold interfaced knot piece in half, right sides together, and machine stitch along edge, leaving ends open. Turn through to right side and press, centring seam on the underside. Place knot piece over gathering line of bow and hand stitch one end down to underside of bow. Turn under opposite end, even the gathers of the bow, and catch down with a few strong, over-sewing stitches to secure the knot.

Cut elastic to fit loosely around the child's neck, plus turnings, then stitch centre of

elastic to reverse side of knot. Neaten and turn under ends and sew on large press stud to fasten at centre back.

4 Wig

Use a buckram or old straw hat shape that fits head closely. Cut one ball of chunky yarn into 20cm lengths. Using three lengths together fold in half and with matching sewing thread, attach loop end of yarn to hat base with a few firm overcasting stitches. Make the first row about 2.5cm above lower edge, and the second row 5cm above this. For the third row, cut the second ball of yarn into 24cm lengths and use four strands together, again securing the loops in a row about 5cm above the previous one. Fill in remaining small circle at centre of crown with a few short tufts of the same yarn.

Face make-up

1 Apply the white foundation cream, using a damp sponge to spread it smoothly and evenly. Cover the entire face, from around the jawline up to the hairline. On small children, avoid taking the make-up under the eyes so as not to get any in the eyes themselves.

2 To set the foundation make-up pat gently with white face powder, to give an even matt finish. Brush away the surplus with a clean, soft make-up brush, ready for applying the clown's features.

3 Using bright red lipstick, paint in solid half-circles over the eyelids and above the natural eyebrows, making the outlines firm and clear. Then add a circle around the tip of the nose, and a wide grin around the mouth, extending the curves over the cheeks, as shown in the illustration below.

4 Outline the mouth with black kohl pencil, and then draw in arched eyebrows on the forehead. Add black crosses over the eyelids to complete the effect.

14

High Wire Act

Just the outfit to make you walk on air, this pretty tight-rope walker's costume has a brief little bra and tutu sparkling with sequins. It is worn with ballet slippers highlighted with net pompons. An irresistible feather head-dress adds the crowning touch.

You will need
For an outfit to fit ages 6-9 (chest size 62cm)

2m of 90cm-wide bright pink net
80cm of 115cm-wide iridescent nylon organza
20cm of 115cm-wide pink lining
Matching sewing threads
2m of pink bias binding
1m of 5mm-wide flat elastic
1m of 2cm-wide elastic
Three hooks and eyes
Small piece of touch-and-close fastener
Box of pink sequins and fabric adhesive
Feathers for head-dress
Dressmaker's pattern paper

Make-up
Pale pink foundation cream and face powder
Pink pearlized eye shadow
Deep pink lipstick

Accessories
White tights
White or pink ballet shoes plus 3m of
   2cm-wide pink satin ribbon for ties
150cm length of narrow dowel or cane for
   balancing pole

Preparing the pattern
Using dressmaker's pattern paper, scale up the pattern pieces given on page 18. 1.5cm seam allowances are included on the bra, unless otherwise stated. Mark in notches, dots and straight grain lines.

The skirt (which is left open at the back) the pompons, straps and the headband are all made from straight pieces of fabric, so paper patterns are not needed.

To cut out
Fold the iridescent fabric in half with selvedges together along one side, and pin the bra pieces in place as shown in the cutting layout. Cut out, noting that loop piece is cut from single fabric. Place relevant pattern pieces onto lining, following same layout. Cut out. Transfer markings.

From the remaining fabric, cut two straight pieces across the width, each 25cm deep, for the outer layer of the skirt. The spare fabric will be needed for the head-band and straps. See layouts, page 18.

From the net, cut one strip 25cm by 2m, and two strips, each 20cm by 2m. Keep the remaining net for pompons.

Sewing instructions
1 Skirt
Place the two 20cm-wide strips of net together, with edges level. Onto these lay the 25cm-wide net strip, and then place on top the strip of iridescent fabric, overlapping excess at centre and ends.

With right sides together, apply bias binding along one long edge, for waist casing. Stitch the binding in place through all layers and turn the full depth of the binding to the wrong side. Machine stitch lower edge of binding to form the casing. Thread narrow elastic through the casing and stitch across one end to secure. Pull up other end of elastic to form gathers, and to fit the waist firmly. Adjust the gathers evenly across the skirt. Stitch other end of elastic to secure and neaten ends. Stitch a small patch of touch-and-close fastener to the inside and outside corners of back waist to

PATTERN

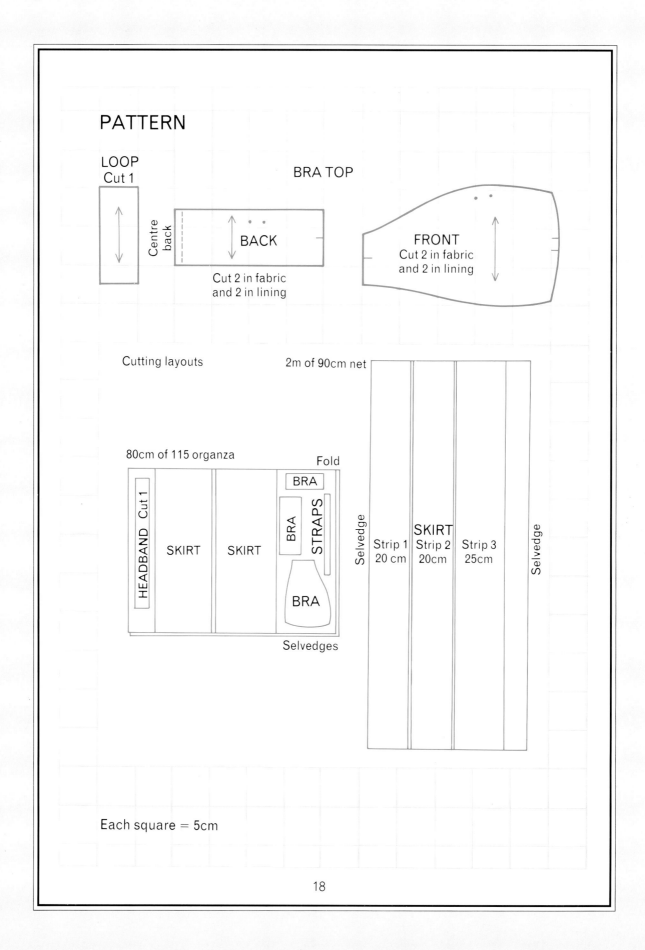

LOOP
Cut 1

BRA TOP

Centre back

BACK

Cut 2 in fabric
and 2 in lining

FRONT
Cut 2 in fabric
and 2 in lining

Cutting layouts

2m of 90cm net

80cm of 115 organza

Fold

HEADBAND Cut 1

SKIRT

SKIRT

BRA

BRA

STRAPS

BRA

Selvedges

Selvedge

SKIRT

Strip 1
20 cm

Strip 2
20cm

Strip 3
25cm

Selvedge

Each square = 5cm

wrap and fasten. Stitch a hook and eye in place for additional strength.

2 Bra top

With right sides together, join centre front seam of bra front pieces, clip into curve and press seam open. Repeat on the corresponding lining pieces. Press 1.5cm turnings to the wrong side on each side edge.

On bra back pieces (both main fabric and lining) turn under 1.5cm to wrong side on one short end of each piece. These will be at the centre back. Place the layers right sides together, and stitch along both long sides. Turn through and press. Cut two pieces of 2cm-wide elastic, each 15cm long, and insert through back piece. One end of elastic should be level with the raw edge, and the other should be pulled through until it extends 1.5cm beyond the folded centre back edges. Pin to hold, then machine stitch the side edge through all thicknesses, close to raw edges. Make a second row of stitching, along the seamline. Stitch the other end through all thicknesses, 5mm from centre back folded edge. Trim excess elastic close to the stitching line, inside the folded edge. Slip-stitch edges together.

Insert the double-stitched, raw edge of the bra back into the folded edge of the bra front, and edge-stitch, through all layers.

Repeat for other side of back. Sew hooks and eyes in place so that the bra will wrap and fasten at centre back.

Fold loop piece lengthways in half, with right sides together, and, taking a 1cm seam, stitch long edge. Turn through, press. Place loop right side up, over centre front of bra. Overlap the ends on the wrong side, pull slightly to pleat, before stitching to secure.

Fold shoulder straps lengthways in half, right sides together, and, taking 1cm turnings, stitch long sides. Turn through, press.

Turn short ends under for 1cm and hand-sew in place to top edge of bra at dots marked, adjusting length at back to fit.

3 Head-dress

Cut a length of 2cm-wide elastic to fit around head, plus an overlap for stitching. From main fabric, cut a straight strip, 6cm-wide by elastic length plus 5cm. Press under 5mm at short ends of strip. With right sides together, stitch long side. Turn through to right side and press. Insert elastic and machine stitch 5mm in from one end, to secure elastic. Repeat for other end, then bring the two ends together for centre back, and stitch together. Sew feathers inside band, as preferred.

4 Pompons

For each pompon: cut three strips of net, each 4cm by 30cm. Place together and gather one long side through all layers. Pull up tightly and fasten off, stitching together to form a circle. Cut two pieces of elastic to fit around foot. Join ends, then sew joining to reverse side of pompon.

5 Sequins

For a pretty, twinkling effect, decorate the surfaces of the entire costume with sequins. Attach them using fabric adhesive.

Face make-up

Apply as for the flower fairy (see page 36).

Rodeo Show

Bareback rider, marksman, showman – if you have a junior Buffalo Bill on your hands, here's the perfect outfit. The shimmering white satin cowboy shirt and trousers sparkle with diamanté studs and motifs picked out in silvery sequins. Silky fringing adds an authentic western touch.

You will need

For an outfit to fit ages 6-9 (length of trousers about 76cm; length of top about 54cm)

2.50m of 115cm-wide white polyester satin
3m of 12cm-deep fringing
Matching sewing thread
70cm of 2cm-wide elastic
Dressmaker's pattern paper
4mm-diameter rhinestone or diamanté studs (about 350 were used for our outfit)
Sequin motifs in silver leaf shapes
Fabric adhesive

Make-up

Black kohl pencil
Deep pink blusher

Accessories

White cowboy hat
White belt
Toy silver pistols

Preparing the pattern

Using dressmaker's pattern paper, scale up the pattern pieces given on page 22. Hems of 3cm and 1.5cm seam allowances are included throughout. Mark in all notches, straight-grain lines, dots and fringe positions on both the front and back top and trouser pattern pieces.

Cutting out

Fold the fabric in half with the selvedges together along one side. Pin the pattern pieces in place as shown in the cutting layout given on page 23, noting that the neck facing is cut from single fabric, and cut out. Place the collar piece to a fold, as shown, and cut out two pieces. Transfer all dots and notches to both layers of fabric, before removing the pattern pieces.

Sewing instructions
1 Trousers

These are stitched with right sides together throughout. Machine right leg front to right leg back along inner leg seam. Repeat for the left leg, and press seams open. With the inner leg seams and notches matching, join the crotch seam from back to front waist edges. Trim curved seam to 6mm, and press it open.

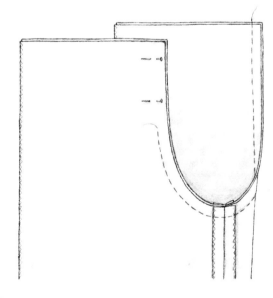

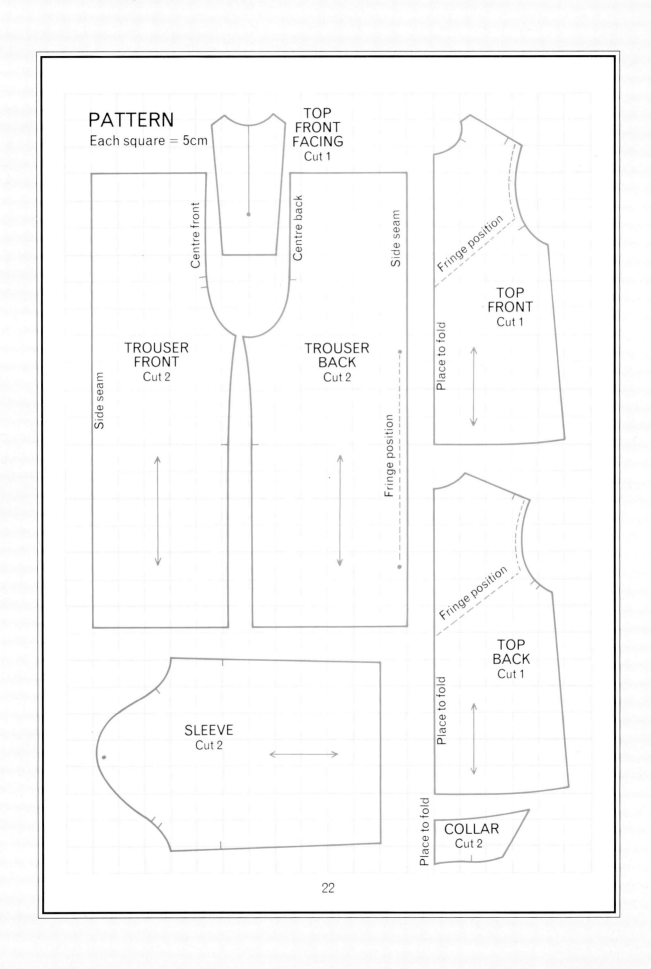

PATTERN
Each square = 5cm

TOP FRONT FACING
Cut 1

Centre front

Centre back

Side seam

TROUSER FRONT
Cut 2

Side seam

TROUSER BACK
Cut 2

Fringe position

Fringe position

Place to fold

TOP FRONT
Cut 1

Fringe position

Place to fold

TOP BACK
Cut 1

SLEEVE
Cut 2

Place to fold

COLLAR
Cut 2

22

On the right side of the fabric, tack a length of fringing to the outside leg pieces between the dots marked, making sure the edges are straight and that the loops of the fringe are facing inwards. Join the trousers together at the side seams, taking care not to catch the fringe in the stitching. Press the seams open.

through the casing. Draw up the elastic, overlap the ends and sew firmly together. Slip-stitch the opening closed.

At the lower edge of trouser legs, turn under 5mm to wrong side and edge-stitch in place. Turn a further 2.5cm to wrong side, or amount required for the correct length. Lightly press the lower edge on the wrong side and slip-stitch hem in place.

2 Top

This is stitched with right sides together throughout. On the neck facing, neaten the sides and the lower edge by making a 6mm turning to the wrong side and edge-stitching. To make the neck opening, place the facing onto the front piece, and with centre front lines and neck curves matching, stitch 5mm either side of centre, tapering towards dot. Cut through both layers, between stitching. Snip into seam towards lower point, and turn facing to wrong side. Press on the wrong side. With raw edges together, tack around curved neckline to secure facing.

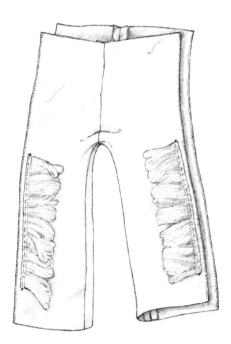

At the waist edge, turn under 5mm to wrong side and edge-stitch in place. Turn under a further 2.5cm to form a casing, and stitch along bottom fold, leaving an opening for the elastic. Cut elastic to fit the waist plus 2.5cm for turnings, and thread it

Cutting layout
2.50m of 115cm fabric

Fold

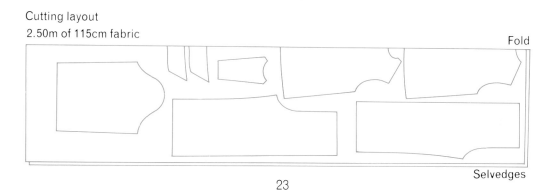

Selvedges

Join front to back along shoulders, and press seams open. Stitch collar pieces together around short ends and un-notched long edge. Clip corners, trim seam, turn through to right side and press. Matching notches and centre front edges, stitch one layer of collar to neckline, and trim seam. Press under seam allowance on other raw edge of collar and slip-stitch in place to previous line of stitching. Press.

Stitch front to back at side seams and press seams open.

Gather top of each sleeve between notches. Join underarm seams of sleeves and press. Pin sleeve into armhole, matching notches, dot to shoulder seam, and sleeve seam to side seam. Draw up gathers to fit, distributing them evenly. Stitch seam, then add a second row of stitching 6mm out from the first. Trim the seam allowance up to second row of stitching, and clip into curves. Press seam. Attach other sleeve.

Make hems of the required depth on sleeves and lower edges of top as for the trouser legs.

Using the dashed line on the pattern as a guide, and starting at the centre back, pin and then hand-stitch the fringing in place across the back, over shoulder line and across the front.

Decorate the top and trousers with a border of rhinestone studs. Add sequins – arranged as in the photograph – or as desired. Stick them in place, using fabric adhesive sparingly, on the point of a tooth-pick or matchstick.

Face make-up

1 Using a very soft kohl pencil, emphasize the natural eyebrows by working over them with short strokes until they are thick-looking and dark.

2 Again using kohl, sketch in a thin moustache lightly, to get the correct shape, then fill in with solid black.

3 Using a soft brush, apply the deep pink blusher to give the effect of full, rounded cheeks.

4 Draw in sideburns with the black kohl pencil, following the natural direction of the hair and fill in with solid colour.

Roll up, Roll up!

Dramatic scarlet and black are used for this splendid ringmaster's outfit. The traditional red tailcoat is trimmed with epaulettes edged with gold braid and fringing and is made from satin, as are the smart spotted cravat and the gleaming jodhpurs. Make the whip, add boots and a black top hat, and your showman is ready for the grand opening performance!

You will need

For an outfit to fit ages 6-9 (jacket length 56cm, trouser length 80cm)

1.80m of 115cm-wide scarlet acetate satin
1.80m of white acetate satin
30cm of 115cm-wide black/white spot satin
30cm of 115cm-wide white satin lining
Matching sewing threads
One gilt button
Pack of adhesive bonding web
70cm of 2cm-wide elastic
1m of 1cm-wide nylon boning
1.10m of 2.5cm-wide white bias binding
25cm by 18cm piece of black felt
25cm by 18cm piece of heavy buckram
60cm of 90cm-wide bonded interfacing
Fabric adhesive
1m of 1cm-wide gold braid
60cm gold fringing
15cm length of touch-and-close fastener
Dressmaker's pattern paper
45cm of 1cm-diameter dowelling, painted black
2 pairs of 90cm-long black leather laces
Clear adhesive

Make-up

Rosy pink foundation cream
Deep pink blusher
Black kohl pencil

Accessories

Black top hat
White gloves
Riding boot-style Wellingtons

Preparing the pattern

Using dressmaker's pattern paper, scale up the pattern pieces given on page 28. 1.5cm seam allowances are included throughout with 2cm hem allowances on the sleeves, and 1.5cm on the jacket. Mark all balance points, (dots) notches, straight-grain and fold lines onto the pattern pieces.

Cutting out

Fold the fabrics in half, with selvedges level along one side. Place pattern pieces as shown in the cutting layouts, noting that the front jacket should be turned to the reverse side (face down) so that it fits in. Pin the pieces in place, with the arrows matching the straight grain, and cut out. Transfer all dots and notches to both layers of fabric.

From bonded interfacing, cut out the jacket front facing, as shown in the layout.

Cut out four pieces each from the black felt and buckram, as in the cutting layout.

Sewing instructions
1 Jacket

This is stitched with right sides together throughout. As satin frays badly, neaten all raw edges with machine zigzag stitching, and tack seams before machining to prevent slipping.

On the jacket fronts, reinforce the inner corners between the shoulder and neck by machine-stitching around the angle, on the seamline, 4cm either side of dot A. Clip into the corners, right up to the stitching. Do the same on the jacket front facings.

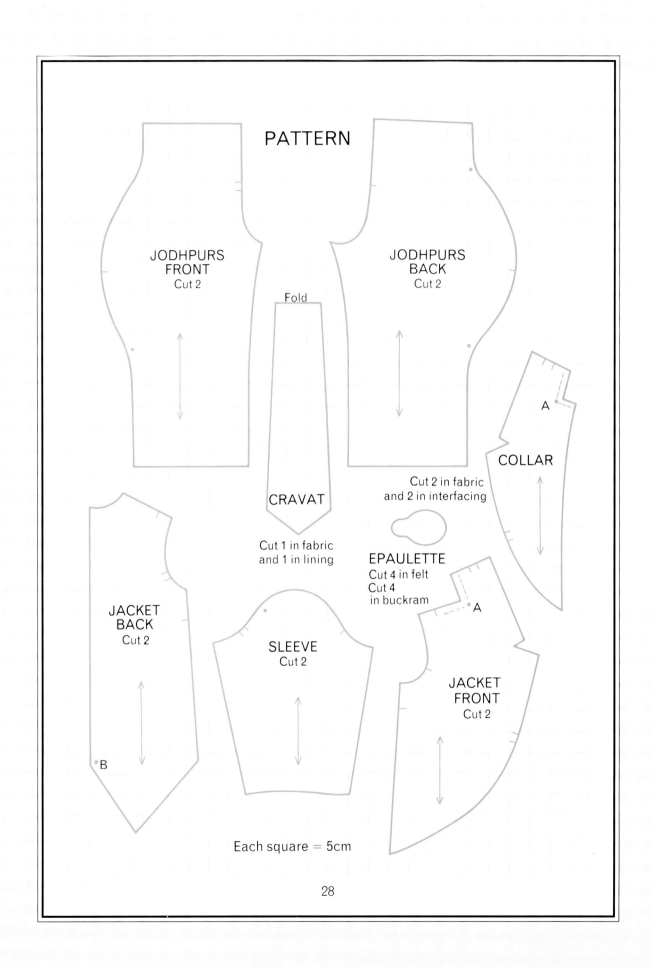

PATTERN

JODHPURS
FRONT
Cut 2

JODHPURS
BACK
Cut 2

Fold

CRAVAT

Cut 1 in fabric
and 1 in lining

Cut 2 in fabric
and 2 in interfacing

A

COLLAR

EPAULETTE
Cut 4 in felt
Cut 4
in buckram

JACKET
BACK
Cut 2

B

SLEEVE
Cut 2

A

JACKET
FRONT
Cut 2

Each square = 5cm

Matching the notches, join centre back seams of front pieces and press them open. (This part forms the under-collar.)

On jacket back pieces, stitch centre seam to dot B and press the seam open. Matching centre back seam of under-collar to centre seam of jacket back, join front to back at shoulders and across the back neckline,

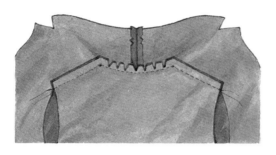

easing them to fit, and pivoting at point A. Clip into seam allowance around neck curve, and press the seam upwards, onto the under-collar.

Tack interfacing to wrong sides of front facings. Turn under inner edge for 6mm and stitch, to neaten. Join centre back neck seam of facing; press seam open. Place facing onto jacket and, matching notches and centre back seams, tack together all round outer edge of collar and fronts. Stitch,

remove tacks and clip into corner of collar. Trim away excess turnings from collar and revers points. Clip into curves, and trim seam allowances in layers. Turn facing to inside, and press edges. At neckline and shoulders, turn under raw edge of facing and slip-stitch in place to previous stitching line.

2 Sleeves

For sleeves, gather between the dots. Matching notches, pin sleeves to armhole edges, pulling up gathers to fit. Tack and stitch sleeves in place. Remove tacks and press seam towards sleeve. Stitch each side seam and under-sleeve seam in one operation. Press seams open. To finish the sleeve hem, turn under 5mm and stitch. Turn under a further 1.5cm, press and slip-stitch the hems in place.

Turn under and press 1.5cm all round lower edge of jacket, mitring corners on tails. The hem may be invisibly stuck in place using iron-on bonding web, where strips are cut to the appropriate width and slipped inside the pressed hem. Following the manufacturer's instructions, press hem to fuse. Alternatively, slip-stitch the hem.

On the left front, just below the roll of the revers, make a stitched buttonhole to fit button size. Sew button in place on to right front, at corresponding position.

Cutting layouts

1.80m of 115cm scarlet satin

30cm of 115cm black/white spot satin
30cm of 115cm satin lining

18cm by 25cm felt and buckram

1.80m of 115cm white satin

60cm of 90cm interfacing

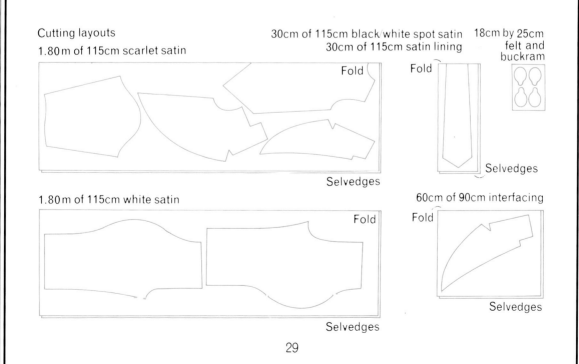

3 Epaulettes

For each epaulette, stick two pieces of buckram or card together, and then stick black felt pieces to each side, to make a pair. For the decoration, stick a strip of narrow gold braid in an S shape to the centre of each epaulette. Surround this with a second strip of braid, applied close to the edge. Finish off by sticking the fringing in place around the curved outside edges. To fasten the epaulettes, stitch one strip of touch-and-close fastener along the centre of the undecorated side, and sew the other half to the shoulder seam of the jacket.

4 Cravat

Open out cravat and lining pieces and place them right sides together. Stitch around, leaving an opening along one long side for turning through. Trim seam allowances, and snip away corners. Turn through to right side and press. With matching thread, slip-stitch opening closed.

5 Jodhpurs

These are stitched with right sides together throughout. Neaten all raw edges. With notches matching, join right leg front to right leg back along inner leg seam; repeat for left leg and press seams open. Matching notches, join the crotch seam, from back to front waist edges. Trim seam around curve to 6mm and press open. Matching dots and notches, stitch side seams; clip curve and press seams open. Press under 5mm around waist edge and edge-stitch in place.

Turn under a further 2.5cm, to form a casing, and stitch along the bottom fold, leaving an opening for the elastic. Cut

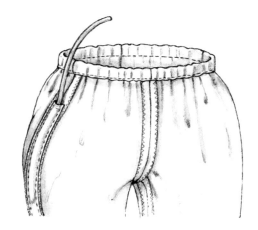

elastic to waist size plus 2.5cm for turnings, and thread it through the casing. Draw up the elastic, overlap ends and sew them firmly together. Slip-stitch opening closed.

At the lower edge of the legs, turn and stitch the hems as for the waistline but without leaving an opening. Press on the wrong side under a dry pressing cloth.

To stiffen the curved side seams, make a casing by stitching bias binding to the wrong side, over each seam, starting and finishing at the dots. Turn under cut edges of binding and stitch across one short end on each side. Cut the nylon boning into two equal pieces, and insert one piece into each casing. If necessary, trim excess boning, and stitch across open end of binding, to close. To further emphasize the fullness, soft, teased-out wadding can always be placed inside the jodhpurs to fill out the outside leg area.

6 Whip

Glue one end of each of three leather laces to one end of the dowelling. Wrap the fourth lace around the same end of the rod covering the ends of the other laces, and continue to wrap it edge to edge around the dowelling for about 9cm. Glue the end firmly in place. Plait the free laces for 35cm then make an overhand knot to secure the plait leaving the ends loose. Make small knots close to the ends of each lace.

Face make-up

1 Apply the rosy coloured foundation cream, covering the entire face. Fade it out towards the hairline and jawline.

2 Lightly pat or brush the rosy-pink blusher onto the cheeks, and add a little extra just beneath the eyes.

3 Using a sharpened kohl stick, emphasize the eyebrows by first lightly dotting over the natural hair, then gradually working up to a thicker effect towards the centre.

4 Use the kohl stick to draw in a curly moustache. Lightly sketch in the complete shape, then fill in with black kohl pencil.

Fairytale

Create the magic of midsummer with this exquisite flower fairy dress complete with wings, wand and coronet of flower petals. The separate wrap-over skirt and fly-away sleeves are made from gossamer-light sheers in flower pastel colours, and are worn over a white leotard and tights.

You will need
For an outfit to fit ages 6-9 (finished skirt length about 50cm)

4m of 90cm-wide white net
1.50m of 112cm-wide pink synthetic sheer
1.50m of 112cm-wide white synthetic sheer
1.50m of 112cm-wide green synthetic sheer
80cm of 115cm-wide pearlized fabric
4.50m of white milliner's wire
1m of 1.5cm-wide white tape
2m of 4cm-wide white ribbon
3m of 1.5cm-wide white ribbon
20cm of rigid nylon boning
Small quantity of wadding
Matching sewing threads
80cm of 2.5cm-wide fold-over braid
40cm of 6mm-wide green ribbon
1m of 6mm-wide pink ribbon
4 press studs
Two D-rings
Fabric adhesive
50cm of 5mm wooden dowel
Dressmaker's pattern paper

Make-up
Pale pink foundation cream
Pale pink face powder
Deep pink blusher
Gold eye shadow
Mascara

Accessories
White leotard or T-shirt
White tights (optional)
White ballet shoes

Preparing the pattern
Using dressmaker's pattern paper, scale up the pattern pieces given on page 34. There are no seam allowances or hems, as the edges of the skirt petals and net are left raw.

The skirt and mock sleeves are made on a foundation of straight pieces of net so paper patterns are not required. Layers of petals in varying sizes are subsequently added.

Transfer the instructions given onto each pattern piece. The scallop shapes are a guide to cutting the lower edge of the net skirt; alternatively, this could be cut free-hand into petal shapes if preferred.

Cutting out
Pin the main pattern pieces, for example, the wings, skirt petals and the larger sepals to the appropriate fabrics and cut out. It is advisable to cut out the smaller petals and sepals as they are needed.

For the skirt, cut two rectangles of white net, each measuring 90cm by 2m. For the sleeves, cut four straight strips of white net, each measuring 15cm by 66cm.

Sewing instructions
1 Skirt
Fold each skirt piece lengthways in half to measure 45cm deep by 2m wide. Place the layers evenly together. Mark and cut folded edges into scallops or petal shapes.

Cut a length of fold-over braid to fit waist plus 5cm for an overlap. Mark waist size onto braid. Using double thread to prevent breaking, gather up long edge of net,

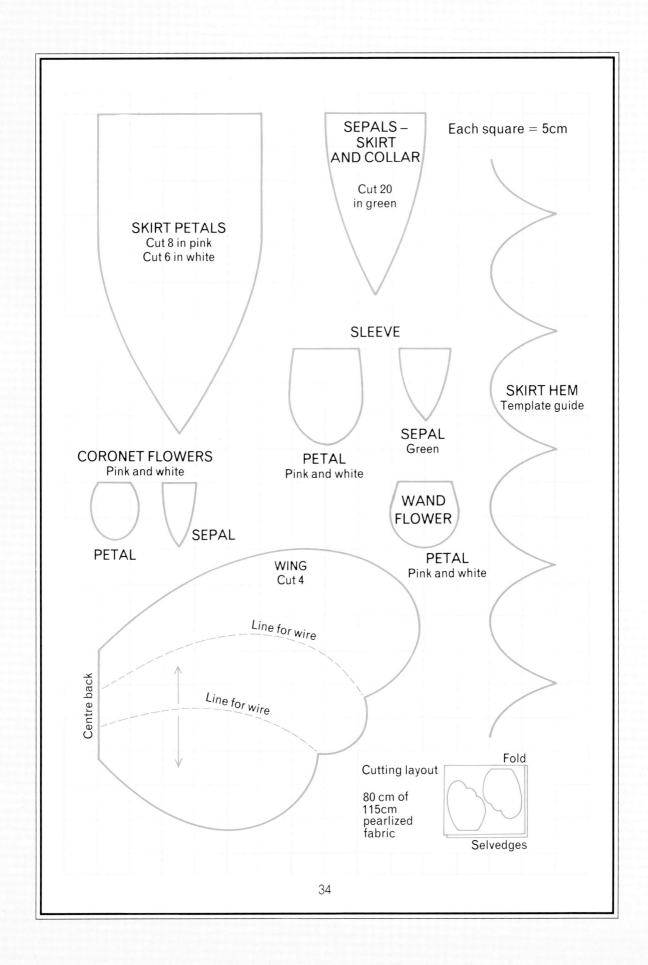

SKIRT PETALS
Cut 8 in pink
Cut 6 in white

SEPALS –
SKIRT
AND COLLAR

Cut 20
in green

Each square = 5cm

SLEEVE

SKIRT HEM
Template guide

SEPAL
Green

CORONET FLOWERS
Pink and white

PETAL
Pink and white

WAND
FLOWER

PETAL

SEPAL

PETAL
Pink and white

WING
Cut 4

Line for wire

Centre back

Line for wire

Cutting layout

80 cm of
115cm
pearlized
fabric

Fold

Selvedges

34

through all layers, and draw up to fit the braid. Bind raw edge of gathers. Sew on two press studs to form centre back wrap.

Stitch skirt petals and sepals in layers, to waist binding, first pleating them along the straight edges. Begin by applying eight skirt petals in pink, then add six skirt petals in white and 12 skirt sepals in green.

2 Collar
Cut a length of green ribbon to fit neck plus 3cm for turnings. Cut out seven collar sepals in green. Pleat each one across the straight edge and stitch evenly to ribbon, leaving 1.5cm free at ends. Turn under excess ribbon and sew on a press stud.

3 Sleeves
For one sleeve, take two pieces of white net 15cm by 66cm. Place together and gather long edge through both layers. Pull up gathers to measure about 5cm and fasten off firmly.

To trim, cut two pink sleeve petals, three in white and five sleeve sepals in green. Pleat or gather straight edges and stitch to the gathered net, starting with the pink and finishing with the green.

Bind the edge as for the skirt waist. Sew a press stud to the bottom corners of the net to fasten edge to edge under the arm. Make a second sleeve in the same way.

When dressing the child catch-stitch centre top point of sleeves to shoulders of leotard to make secure.

4 Coronet
Using milliner's wire, form a firm ring to fit the head, then snip and twist the ends together to secure. Bind wire with tape as a foundation for sewing on flowers.

For each flower: cut a strip of white net 30cm by 5cm. Gather up one long side tightly, to form flower centre. Cut out flower petals: two in pink, four in white plus a strip in green, 15cm long by 7cm deep. Cut one long edge into zigzag shapes, to suggest small sepals. Stitch petals and sepals to back of flower centre, pleating and gathering to create the open flower effect.

Make eight similar flowers and stitch the base of each one to the covered circlet.

5 Wand
Bind the piece of dowel with a long, narrow strip of the green fabric. Cut two strips of net, 7cm by 45cm for the flower centre. Cut out petals using wand petal pattern, as follows: five pink and four white. Make up the flower, gathering the net in the centre, as for the flowers of the coronet.

Attach flower to end of dowel, and add a pink ribbon streamer, if desired.

6 Wings
Make up the two wings separately. On the reverse side of two of the wing pieces, which will become the underside, shape two lengths of wire to fit all round the outer curve of each one, and stick or stitch the wire lightly in place, about 3mm in from raw edge. Shape and glue on two more lengths of wire across each wing where indicated by dashed lines on the pattern.

Place corresponding plain wing pieces on top of each wired section, wrong sides together, and machine stitch around outer edge of wings, close to the wire. Make similar lines of stitching to outline the wire, across the wings.

For the harness, cut a piece of 4cm-wide ribbon to twice the length of the centre back edge of wing, plus 2cm. Press short ends under for 1cm, then bring them together, thus halving the length, and stitch together along long edges only. Cut a piece of rigid nylon boning to length of ribbon, cover it with wadding and slip this inside the ribbon tube. Top-stitch the opening closed. Cut the length of narrower ribbon in half, fold two ends under, cross them at right angles and stitch firmly to top end of ribbon tube. At the opposite end, place two D-rings vertically side by side, and oversew to padded tube. Oversew centre back edges of wing halves to plain side of ribbon tube.

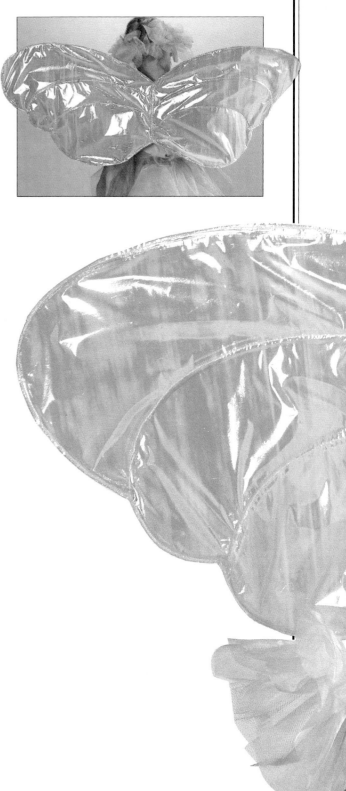

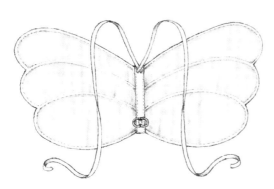

To wear, pass the ribbons over the shoulders, across the chest, through the D-rings and tie in front. Trim surplus ribbon.

Face make-up

1 Apply the pale pink foundation cream evenly over the face, fading it out towards the hair and jawline.

2 Use pale pink face powder to set the foundation, brushing away the surplus with a soft make-up brush.

3 Colour the cheeks lightly with deep pink blusher.

4 Using a soft applicator, brush gold eye shadow onto the eyelids, then darken the lashes with the mascara. For the tight-rope walker, apply pink sequins to the cheeks with a spot of vaseline.

Gone Fishing

This jolly gnome sports a quick-to-sew tunic in shiny PVC-coated cotton over mossy green breeches, with elasticated waist and legs. The boots, like the breeches, are made from green felt and have pointed tops to match the collar of the tunic. The authentic pointed hat, without which no garden gnome would be correctly dressed, is made from green felt, and the bushy beard is cut from wadding.

You will need
For an outfit to fit ages 6-9 (finished length of breeches approx 62cm)

2.20m of 90cm-wide green felt
80cm of 150cm-wide red PVC-coated cotton
46cm by 46cm of red felt
Matching sewing threads
1.50m of 2cm-wide elastic
2.5cm of touch-and-close fastener
Fabric adhesive
50cm of heavy-weight wadding
60cm of milliner's wire
Wire cutters
Small quantity of adhesive tape
Dressmaker's pattern paper

Make-up
Pink foundation cream
Pink face powder
Deep pink blusher
Grey eyeshadow

Accessories
Red long-sleeved T-shirt
Red tights or socks
Brown leather belt
Fishing rod

Preparing the pattern
Using dressmaker's pattern paper, scale up the pattern pieces shown on page 40. For the breeches, copy the pattern given on page 46 for Sinbad's trousers but the shorter length, cutting or folding along the dashed lines, where indicated. Transfer all marks and notches onto each pattern piece.

As this outfit is made from non-fraying fabrics, hems have been allowed on the breeches only, which have 3cm included at the waist and on the legs, for casings to take the elastic.

1.5cm seam allowances are included on the tunic and breeches, and 5mm on the boots and the hat.

Cutting out
For the breeches, boots and collar, fold the felt fabric in half lengthways, with the selvedges together. Pin the pattern pieces in place, following the cutting layout. If you are using a woven fabric, make sure the arrows follow the straight grain. Cut out.

For the tunic, fold the PVC with right sides together and place the pattern piece as shown in the cutting layout, but to avoid making pin holes, do not pin it in place. Simply chalk around the pattern, or secure with masking tape, and cut out.

For the hat, pin the pattern in place onto single felt, as shown in the diagram, and cut out.

Sewing instructions
1 Breeches
These are stitched right sides together throughout. Matching notches, machine together right front and back leg sections

PATTERN

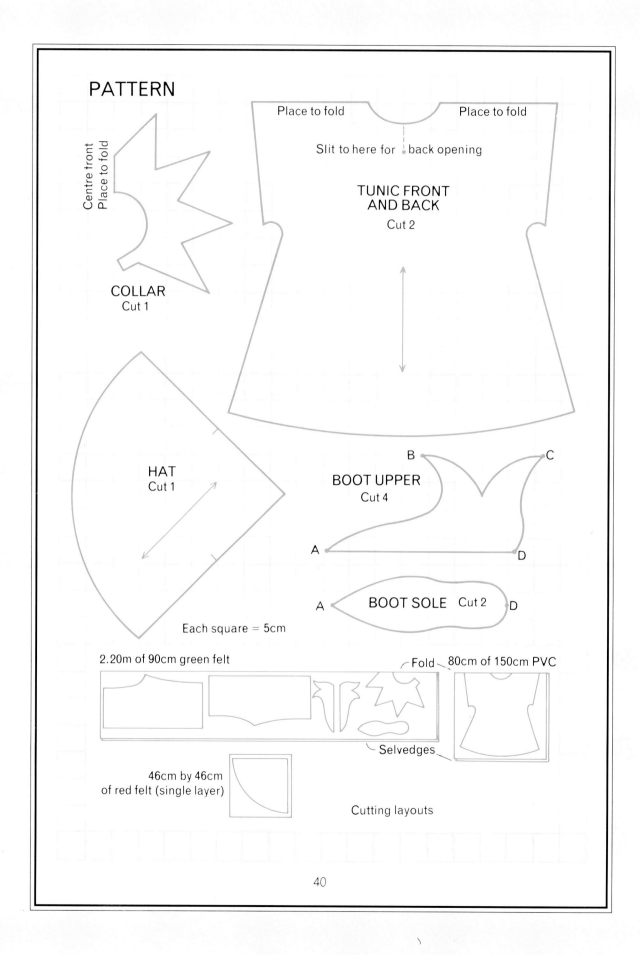

Centre front
Place to fold

COLLAR
Cut 1

Place to fold   Place to fold

Slit to here for ⋮ back opening

TUNIC FRONT
AND BACK
Cut 2

HAT
Cut 1

B   C
BOOT UPPER
Cut 4
A   D

A   BOOT SOLE   Cut 2   D

Each square = 5cm

2.20m of 90cm green felt

Fold   80cm of 150cm PVC

Selvedges

46cm by 46cm
of red felt (single layer)

Cutting layouts

along inner leg seam; repeat for left leg, and press seams open. Matching the notches, join the side seams and press open. Matching the inner leg seams and notches, join the two legs together around crotch seam, from back to front waist. Trim curved seam to 1cm wide, and press open.

At the waist, make a double turning pressing 5mm to the wrong side, then a further 2.5cm. To make the hem casing, machine close to the top and bottom folds, leaving a small gap in the stitching on the lower edge.

Cut a length of elastic to fit the waist plus 2.5cm for turnings. Insert elastic into the casing, and when you have threaded in most of the elastic, pin the loose end to the casing to prevent it from slipping through, then draw it up, overlap the ends and sew firmly together. Slip-stitch the opening closed.

Make similar casings around the lower edges of legs, and then cut and insert pieces of elastic to fit comfortably around the calves.

2 Tunic

Note: if using PVC-coated fabric, do not press with an iron. These plastic fabrics shed creases fairly quickly when hung up in a warm place.

With right sides together, stitch side seams from underarm to hem. Clip into the curved sections, and finger-press seams open. Using fabric adhesive sparingly, stick down the seam allowances so that they lie flat. For the neck opening, make a 5cm slit from the neck edge down the centre back. Try on the tunic and, if necessary, lengthen the slit to fit the child's head. Turn the tunic right side out.

3 Collar

Open out the collar piece, make 1.5cm turnings on the centre back edges and lightly stick down. When the adhesive is dry, stitch small patches of the touch-and-close fastener along the edges so that the collar will wrap and fasten neatly at the back of the neck and sit comfortably on top of the tunic.

4 Boots

(These are seamed edge to edge, on the right side of the fabric.) Place the uppers together in pairs and, taking 5mm seams, join the centre front seam from point A to point B, then join the back seam from point C to point D. Either hand stitch using small running stitches, or machine stitch, lengthening the stitch to account for the thickness of the felt.

Attach each sole to the lower edge of the upper, matching points A and D together. Pad the points of the toes with wadding, leaving the right length for the child's foot to be inserted.

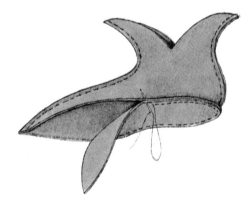

5 Beard

Cut a 42cm length of wire, bend the ends under for 1cm and bind them securely with adhesive tape. Now curve the ends for about 4cm, to form loops to fit over child's ears. Form the wire into a squared U-shape. (see the illustration on the following page) with the base measuring about 8cm across.

Wrap and attach a second length of wire to the lower corners of the U-shape, bending it into an upward curve to make a bridge across the frame for the moustache. Bind the joins with tape. Wrap and stitch narrow strips of wadding around the entire frame to cover the wire.

MOUSTACHE
Trace pattern

For the moustache, trace off the pattern given opposite (actual size), and cut out once in wadding. Place the wire frame centrally onto a 24cm square of wadding, and using the U shape as a guide, cut out the centre part. For a longer beard, increase the wadding to the length required. Stitch the wadding to the frame, try on the beard, and trim to desired shape. Stitch the moustache in place to complete the bearded look.

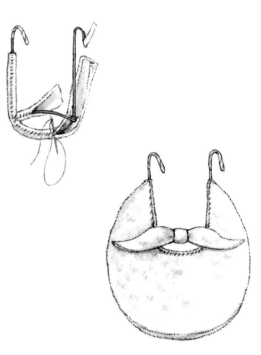

6 Hat
With right sides together, and notches matching, stitch centre back seam, forming cone shaped hat. Lightly press seam open. Turn to right side.

Face make-up
1 Apply pink foundation cream, spreading it evenly over the face, and fading it out towards the hair and jawline.

2 Using a soft make-up brush, make round rosy cheeks with the deep pink blusher, working from the plumpest part of the face outwards.

3 With a soft applicator, darken the eyelids with grey eye shadow, softly blending in the colour towards the eyebrows.

Sinbad the Sailor

Look out for unusual, richly patterned glitter fabrics to create this costume for a swashbuckling sailor. The bolero is cut from shiny brocade and the baggy trousers from striped lurex. These are tied at the waist with a wide, brightly coloured sash of plain-coloured lurex, looped to hold his scimitar.

You will need
For an outfit to fit ages 6-9 (trouser length, 82cm)

50cm of 115cm-wide lurex brocade
2m of 115cm-wide striped lurex lamé
1m of 115cm-wide plain lurex lamé
Matching sewing threads
1.30m of 1cm-wide elastic
Dressmaker's pattern paper

Make-up
Yellow foundation cream
Dark brown face powder
Eye shadow in black and gold
Black kohl pencil
Black mascara

Accessories
Purchased lurex turban (or length of similar fabric could be wound around the head)
Shiny bangles
Toy scimitar

Preparing the pattern
Using dressmaker's pattern paper, scale up the pattern pieces for the trousers and bolero given on page 46. (The sash is made from straight-cut strips so pattern pieces are not given.)

Seam allowances of 1.5cm are included on the trousers and the lined bolero, and 1cm on the sash. 3cm hem allowances are included on the trousers at the waist and on the legs.

Mark in all the notches, straight-grain lines and fold lines.

Cutting out
For the trousers, fold the striped fabric in half lengthways, with selvedges level. Place the pattern pieces as shown in the cutting layout, and cut out. For the bolero, fold the brocade lengthwise in half with the selvedges together, and pin the pattern pieces in place as shown in the cutting layout, and cut out. For the bolero lining and sash, fold the plain fabric as for the brocade, and using the bolero pattern pieces again pin these in position as shown in the lining cutting layout and cut out. From the remaining fabric, mark out two strips for the sash on double fabric each measuring 16cm by 87cm. Cut out.

Sewing instructions
1 Trousers
These are stitched with right sides together throughout. With notches matching, join right leg front to right leg back along inner leg seam; repeat for left leg and press seams open. Matching the notches, join the side seam of each leg, and press seams open. Place one leg inside the other and, matching the inner leg seams and notches, join the crotch seam from back to front waist. Trim the curved seam to 1cm and press open.

At the waist, make a double turning first pressing 5mm to the wrong side, and then a further 2.5cm. Pin and machine close to bottom fold, leaving a small gap in the stitching on the lower edge to insert the elastic. Cut a length of elastic to fit the waist plus 2.5cm for turnings. Insert elastic into

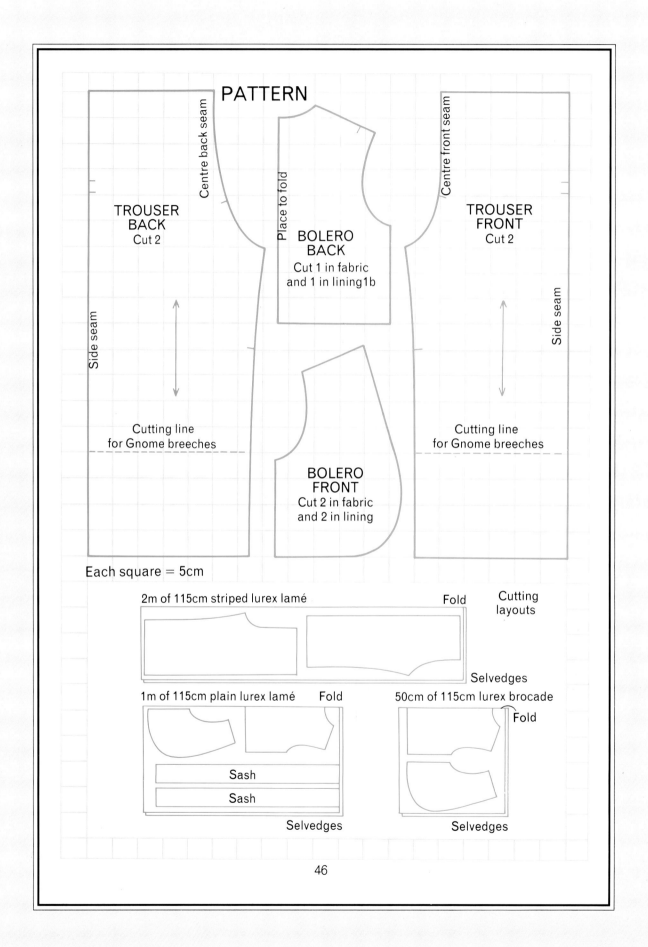

PATTERN

Centre back seam

TROUSER
BACK
Cut 2

Side seam

Cutting line
for Gnome breeches

Place to fold

BOLERO
BACK

Cut 1 in fabric
and 1 in lining1b

BOLERO
FRONT

Cut 2 in fabric
and 2 in lining

Centre front seam

TROUSER
FRONT
Cut 2

Side seam

Cutting line
for Gnome breeches

Each square = 5cm

2m of 115cm striped lurex lamé   Fold   Cutting
layouts

Selvedges

1m of 115cm plain lurex lamé   Fold   50cm of 115cm lurex brocade

Fold

Sash

Sash

Selvedges   Selvedges

two long strips. Press seams open. Place the strips right sides together and stitch around the edge, leaving a small gap along one long side for turning through. Trim seam and corners and turn through to right side. Slip-stitch opening closed and press.

Face make-up

1 Apply yellow foundation cream over the face, neck and chest, and other parts of the body that will show.

2 Pat brown powder over the foundation and brush away the surplus, using a soft make-up brush.

3 Using a black kohl pencil, draw in heavy, arched eyebrows. Mark in lines under the eyes, sweeping them out at the sides.

4 Using a soft applicator, shade in a little black eye shadow around the eye socket, then brush gold powder onto the eyelids and above the socket shadows.

5 Apply mascara to the eye lashes.

6 Using black kohl pencil, mark in a thin moustache with fine lines, then add a small pointed beard.

hem casing, draw it up, overlap the ends and sew firmly together. Slip-stitch the opening closed. Make casings around the legs in the same way, cutting elastic to comfortably fit the ankles.

2 Bolero

With right sides together, join shoulder seams separately of bolero and bolero lining. Place lining onto bolero and stitch together around armholes, inner front edges and around neck in a continuous movement, then across lower back edge, leaving side edges open for turning through. Trim seam allowances, clip into curves and turn to right side. Press seamed edges.

Join the side seams of the bolero only, and press open. Fold under seam allowances on lining fronts. Slip-stitch lining in place, covering raw edges of back lining.

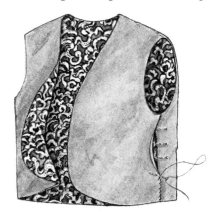

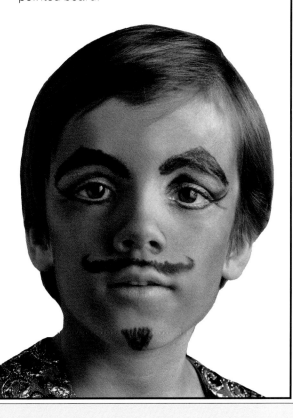

3 Sash

With right sides together, join the short ends of each pair of sash pieces to make

Pretty Princess

This shimmering white-and-gold dress is guaranteed to make any little girl feel like a fairytale princess on her wedding day. The gold train, with its stiffened, stand-up collar is firmly attached to the back neck of the dress, to make movement easy. Glistening pearls and decorative gold braid applied in bands to the front bodice and skirt give the effect of rich embroidery to this magical dress.

You will need
For an outfit to fit ages 6-9 (length of dress, from shoulder, about 92cm)

2.40m of 115cm-wide cream satin
1.10m of 115cm-wide gold lamé
Matching sewing threads
1.20m of 6mm-wide elastic
5m of 1cm-wide gold braid
2m of pearl trim
Small quantity of lightweight wadding
20cm by 40cm piece of buckram
15cm length of touch-and-close fastener
Dressmaker's pattern paper

Make-up
Pale pink foundation cream
Rosy pink blusher
Pink lipstick
Gold eye shadow
Mascara

Accessories
Shoes (satin slippers)
Gold cardboard crown
Pearl necklace
Rings

Preparing the pattern
Using dressmaker's pattern paper, scale up the pattern pieces given on page 54. Mark in all notches, dots, letters A and B, fold lines and straight-grain lines. 1.5cm seams have been allowed, with a 2.5cm hem on the skirt. Note: the train itself is simply a straight rectangle of fabric, so a paper pattern is not required.

Cutting out
For the dress, open the satin to full width and fold it crossways in half with the selvedges level and the fold along the bottom. Following the cutting layout for the dress, cut out the pattern pieces as shown, noting that both bodice and facing pieces must be placed to a fold.

For the train, cut off an 85cm-length, from lamé, across the width. From the remaining lamé, cut out two collar pieces, as shown. Using the collar interfacing pattern, cut out one piece each from buckram and wadding.

Transfer all notches, straight-grain lines and dots to fabric pieces.

Sewing instructions
1 Dress
This is made up with right sides together throughout. With notches matching, join skirt front to skirt back at the sides and press seams open. Gather around top edge stitching 1.5cm from raw edge.

At the top of the sleeve, machine along the seam line, from point A to point A. Clip into the seam allowance at both dots B. Press under 6mm to the wrong side between dots B, then turn under a second time so that machined line is along the upper fold. Stitch close to lower folded

48

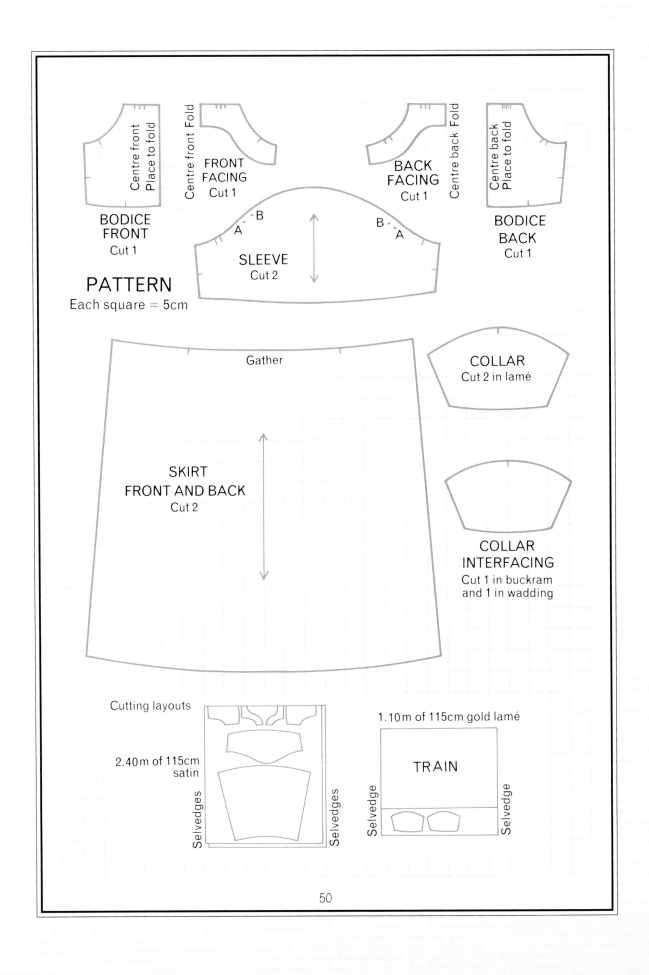

BODICE
FRONT
Cut 1

Centre front
Place to fold

FRONT
FACING
Cut 1

Centre front Fold

BACK
FACING
Cut 1

Centre back Fold

BODICE
BACK
Cut 1

Centre back
Place to fold

B
A

SLEEVE
Cut 2

B
A

PATTERN
Each square = 5cm

Gather

SKIRT
FRONT AND BACK
Cut 2

COLLAR
Cut 2 in lamé

COLLAR
INTERFACING
Cut 1 in buckram
and 1 in wadding

Cutting layouts

2.40m of 115cm
satin

Selvedges

Selvedges

1.10m of 115cm gold lamé

TRAIN

Selvedge

Selvedge

edge, to form a casing. Cut a piece of elastic 12.5cm long and thread it through the casing. Draw it up and secure at both ends, stitching through all thicknesses. Repeat for second sleeve head.

Matching notches, pin and tack sleeves to front bodice, from underarm to point A. On front facing, neaten long, un-notched edge by turning it under for 6mm and stitching close to the fold. With raw edges level, and notches matching, pin, tack and stitch front facing to bodice front around armholes and

across front neckline. Trim seam and corners and clip into curves. Turn the facing over to the inside, and press. Repeat for the back bodice. Matching notches, join bodice front to back at sides, stitching from waist to lower edge of sleeves, catching in turned-down facings. Press seams open. Turn under 6mm around sleeve edge, then a further 1.5cm. Stitch close to lower folded edge to form a casing, leaving a small gap in the stitching. Cut elastic to fit upper arms and thread through casings. Draw up, overlap and stitch ends together.

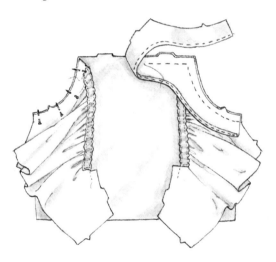

Matching side seams and notches, and with raw edges level, pin skirt to bodice at waist. Draw up gathers to fit bodice, and secure thread. Tack and stitch waistline seam. To form a waistline casing for a more snug fit, work a second row of stitching through the turnings only, close to the raw edges, leaving a gap in the stitching at one side seam. Cut a length of elastic to fit child's waist plus a 2.5cm overlap, and insert through the casing. Draw up, overlap the ends and stitch firmly together. Slip-stitch the opening closed. Zigzag top raw edge of waist seam, to neaten. Remove all tacking threads.

Turn under 5mm to wrong side around lower edge of skirt, and stitch. Turn under a further 2cm and lightly slip-stitch the hem in place. Press.

Following the illustration above, hand-sew lines of gold braid and pearl trim from front neckline to hem, then across the bodice and skirt, as desired, increasing the depth between each row, as shown in the diagram. Tuck the raw ends of the shorter pieces under the outer trim to neaten.

51

2 Train

(If the selvedges are neat, leave the outer edges of the train unfinished. If not, turn them under singly, and stitch.) Gather across train piece, 1.5cm in from one raw edge. Turn and stitch a single 1.5cm hem to the right side at other end of the train. Sew a gold braid over this turned-up edge.

For the stand-up collar, stitch the two collar pieces with right sides together, leaving the lower edge open, as shown on the pattern. Trim corners and turn through. Press. Insert the buckram and then the wadding into the collar (the wadded side becomes the top collar). Join the edge of the

under-collar right sides together to neck edge of train, drawing up the gathers to fit the collar. Turn under opposite edge of collar along seamline and slip-stitch in place to the previous row of stitching. Sew gold braid to inner edge of top collar.

To attach the train to the back of the dress, stitch a piece of touch-and-close fastener centrally to the outside neckline, and the opposite half to the centre of the top collar, immediately above the gathers.

Face make-up

1 Apply the pale pink foundation cream, spreading it evenly over the face and fading it out towards the hair and jawline.

2 Colour the cheeks with pink blusher.

3 Apply pink lipstick, following the natural outline of the lips.

4 Using a soft applicator, brush gold eye shadow onto the eyelids.

5 Darken the upper and lower lashes preferably with deep brown mascara.

Good Knight

Silver lamé and diamond mesh net are cleverly used to create the armour for this brave knight. His shield is of stiff card, sprayed with silver and decorated with felt symbols, and his realistic helmet with three magnificent felt plumes on top, is made from card and buckram, similarly sprayed. Add a toy sword, and our hero is armed and ready for battle from head to toe.

You will need
For an outfit to fit ages 6-9

1.40m of 115cm-wide poly/cotton in white
2m of 115cm-wide diamond-mesh net in silver
70cm of 115cm-wide silver lamé
50cm of 90cm-wide buckram
Large sheet of stout card
20cm of 90cm-wide heavy bonded interfacing
30cm by 24cm piece of grey felt
23cm by 20cm piece of bright red·felt
65cm by 55cm piece of bright blue felt
Matching sewing threads
Fabric adhesive
70cm of grey bias binding
One hook and eye
36cm of touch-and-close fastener in white
70cm of 90cm-wide lightweight wadding
1.50m of cotton-covered wire
100 plastic screw head covers (as rivets on helmet and shield)
Metallic silver spray paint
Paper glue
Dressmaker's pattern paper

Make-up
Face powder in grey and two shades of brown
Black kohl pencil

Accessories
Grey tights
Silver lurex gloves
White belt
Toy sword

Preparing the pattern
Using dressmaker's pattern paper, scale up the pattern pieces given on page 56. To obtain patterns for the blue and red felt trims, trace off the chevrons and one circle from the tunic and shield patterns.

1.5cm turnings have been allowed on all seams. Mark in notches, dots, dart on balaclava, tab positions on tunic plus the fold and straight-grain lines.

Cutting out
Following the cutting layouts given overleaf, open the white fabric to full width and re-fold in half with a fold at the top, and with the selvedges together at the sides. Place the tunic and tab pieces onto the fabric, as shown, and cut out. Open the silver lamé and fold as for the white fabric before cutting out the gauntlet and shoe pieces which must go to a fold, as shown. Fold the silver mesh fabric in half lengthwise and pin the balaclava and shirt pattern pieces on the doubled fabric, and cut out. From the felt pieces, cut out the chevrons, circles and outer soles in the appropriate colours, as shown in the layouts. From buckram, cut out the helmet rectangle, a 19.5cm-diameter circle for the helmet crown, a plume-holder and a pair of inner soles. From heavy interfacing cut the shoe stiffeners. From wadding, cut out two shoe pieces and two from the gauntlet pattern.

Transfer all pattern markings onto the appropriate fabrics. (Instructions for cutting out the shield from card follow in step 8.)

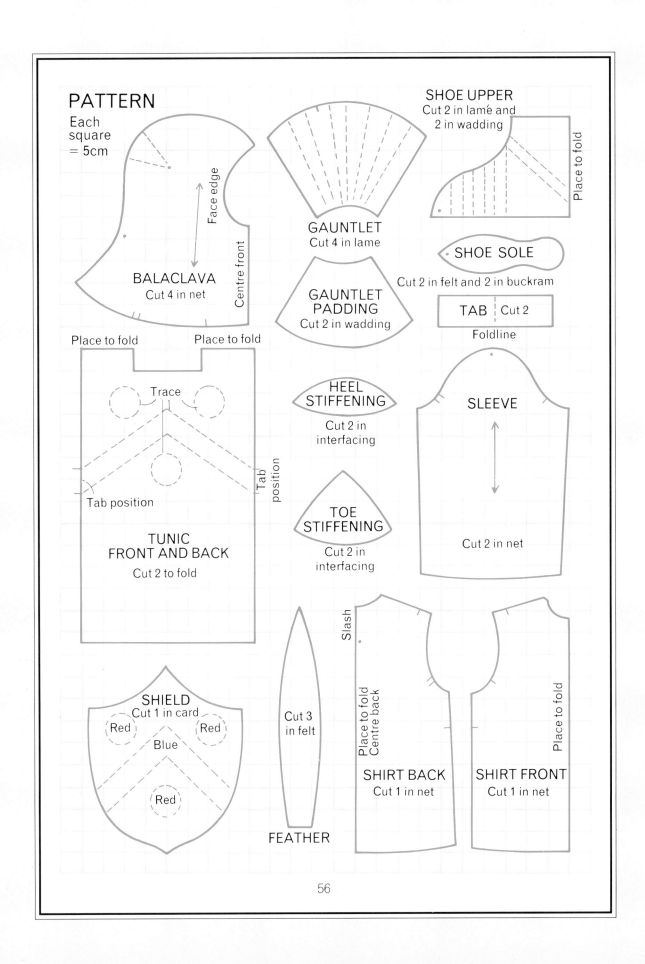

PATTERN

Each square = 5cm

BALACLAVA
Cut 4 in net

Face edge

Centre front

GAUNTLET
Cut 4 in lame

GAUNTLET PADDING
Cut 2 in wadding

SHOE UPPER
Cut 2 in lamé and
2 in wadding

Place to fold

SHOE SOLE

Cut 2 in felt and 2 in buckram

TAB | Cut 2

Foldline

HEEL STIFFENING

Cut 2 in interfacing

TOE STIFFENING

Cut 2 in interfacing

SLEEVE

Cut 2 in net

Place to fold   Place to fold

Trace

Tab position

Tab position

TUNIC FRONT AND BACK

Cut 2 to fold

SHIELD
Cut 1 in card

Red   Red

Blue

Red

Cut 3 in felt

FEATHER

Slash

Place to fold
Centre back

SHIRT BACK
Cut 1 in net

Place to fold

SHIRT FRONT
Cut 1 in net

Cutting layouts

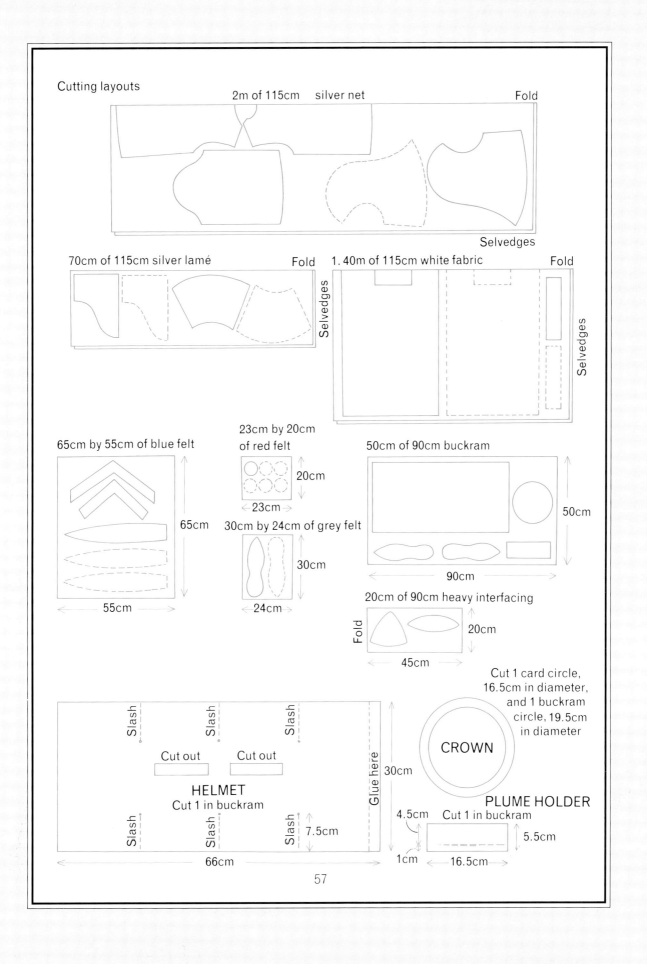

2m of 115cm   silver net   Fold

Selvedges

70cm of 115cm silver lamé   Fold   1.40m of 115cm white fabric   Fold

Selvedges

Selvedges

65cm by 55cm of blue felt

23cm by 20cm
of red felt

50cm of 90cm buckram

20cm

23cm

65cm

30cm by 24cm of grey felt

30cm

50cm

55cm

24cm

90cm

20cm of 90cm heavy interfacing

Fold

20cm

45cm

Cut 1 card circle,
16.5cm in diameter,
and 1 buckram
circle, 19.5cm
in diameter

Slash   Slash   Slash

CROWN

Cut out   Cut out

Glue here

30cm

HELMET
Cut 1 in buckram

PLUME HOLDER

Slash   Slash   Slash

7.5cm

4.5cm   Cut 1 in buckram

5.5cm

66cm   1cm   16.5cm

Sewing instructions
1 Tunic

This is stitched with right sides together throughout. Fold the tab pieces in half with short ends together, and stitch along both long sides. Trim seams and turn through. Press. Open out one tunic piece flat, right side up, and with tabs lying inwards and raw edges level, tack tabs to side edges of front tunic, at positions marked on the pattern. Place second opened-out tunic piece on top, right side down, and matching raw edges, stitch together at sides and lower edge of tunic front, only. Trim seams and turn through. Fold under raw edges along lower edge of back, and edge-stitch through all thicknesses, to close. Press. Clip corners of neckline diagonally, to seam-line, on both layers. Turn the seam allowances of neck edge in towards each other and edge-stitch through all thicknesses. Press on the wrong side.

Place the red felt circles and blue chevron centrally onto the tunic front and stitch them in place, close to the edges. Attach a 3cm-long strip of touch-and-close fastener to inside end of each tab, and sew the matching halves to corresponding positions on outside back edge of tunic, to fasten.

2 'Chain-mail' shirt

This is stitched with right sides together throughout. Matching notches, stitch front to back at the shoulders and side seams. Press seams open. To make a neck opening, cut along centre back fold from neck edge to dot. Try on for fit. Bind the back opening with bias binding. Bind around the neck edge in the same way, turning ends of binding under at centre back of neck, to neaten. Sew a hook and eye to top of opening to fasten edge to edge.

To neaten lower raw edge of shirt, turn it under for 1.5cm and stitch the hem in place. Press on the wrong side.

Stitch sleeve seams and press them open. Gather tops of sleeves between the notches. Turn sleeves right side out and, with notches matching, insert sleeves into armholes, with dot on sleeve to shoulder seam, pull up gathering thread and tack and stitch in place. To neaten lower edge of each sleeve, turn them under for 1.5cm and then stitch hems in place. Press.

3 Balaclava

This is stitched with right sides together throughout. On wrong side, stitch a dart at marked positions, on all four hood pieces. Trim darts and press. Stitch two matching hood pieces together, around face edge only. Repeat for other two pieces. Trim and clip seams to stitching. With the half-hoods still inside out, join a centre front edge of each half together, on the upper and under layer, so that there are two separate centre front seams. Press open. Matching these seamlines stitch around lower edge of hood between dots. Clip seams to dot. Trim seam allowance, and corners, then turn through to right side. Fold hood in half, matching dots and stitch centre back together, through all thicknesses. Neaten seam.

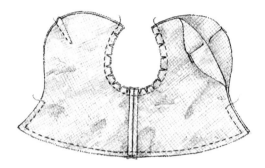

4 Gauntlets

Place the lamé gauntlet pieces with right sides together, in pairs, and stitch along sides and around outward (top) curve. Trim seams and corners and turn right side out. Clip around curved lower edge. Place padding inside gauntlets, turn under lower edges for 1.5cm and edge-stitch close to folds. Top-stitch 3mm in, all round edges of each one. With matching thread, quilt along the lines indicated and then stitch strips of touch-and-close fastener to inside and outside side edges, to wrap and fasten.

5 Shoes

Make as for Space Invader (see page 85)

6 Shield

Cut out shield shape from stout card. Cut a strip of card measuring 20cm by 3.5cm and stick ends in place, to centre back of shield piece, for a handle. On the outside, stick the screw head covers, to represent rivets, all round outer edge. Spray entire front with silver paint. When dry stick the blue chevron and red circles of felt in place.

7 Helmet
On buckram helmet piece cut out oblong eye holes, then cut slits along top and bottom edges, as shown on pattern diagram. Overlap slits on top edge by 2.5cm and glue in position. Overlap slits along bottom edge by 1.5cm and glue in position. Bring side edges together to form a cylinder, overlap them for 2.5cm and glue down, for centre back. When dry, cut down centre back for 12.5cm from top edge, overlap for a further 2.5cm and glue edges in place. Repeat at bottom edge of centre back, but make the cut only 7.5cm long before overlapping 2.5cm as before. For crown of helmet, cut out a 16.5cm- diameter circle in card and stick it down centrally onto buckram crown piece, with 1.5cm turning all round. Clip edge of buckram circle, up to card, and glue clipped edge (buckram side up) to top edge of helmet.

Cut enough card strips, 4cm-wide by depth of helmet, to cover vertical 'darts' and stick in place. Cut and stick 2cm-wide strips of card around outside edges of eye-holes, and around top and bottom edges of helmet.

To make the plume holder, bring short ends of the buckram strip together, overlap them for 2.5cm and glue together. Clip around lower edge, and, folding the clipped edge outwards, stick the underside down to centre top of crown. Cut a ring of buckram and stick over plume holder, to neaten raw

edge. Stick 'studs' around top, bottom edges and along vertical strips. Spray the entire helmet silver.

For the plumes, stick lengths of covered wire along centre of each felt piece, and fold them in half with wire inside. Make diagonal

snips along double edge of each plume to look like feathers. Pleat the straight ends and glue these ends into plume holder.

Face make-up
1 Apply the natural foundation cream, spreading it evenly over the entire face.
Cover the foundation with lighter brown powder, brushing away the surplus with a soft make-up brush.

2 Using a soft eye shadow applicator, and darker brown powder, accentuate areas where natural wrinkles occur. Shade in lines at the sides of the nose, under the eyes and mouth, softening the edges with a fingertip.

3 Thicken the eyebrows with black kohl pencil, and then draw in a thick moustache.

4 Using a soft applicator and grey powder, touch up the eyes by drawing a line just beneath the lower lashes.

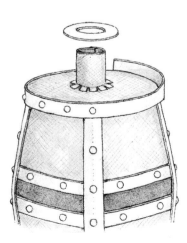

Jungle Cat

Realistic, tiger-striped fur fabric is used to make this body-suit-with-a-difference. The body is fastened at the front with a zip, and the hood, lined with felt and complete with ears, is separate. So that the outfit looks all of one piece, the boots and mittens are cut from the same fabric, with brown felt pads and soles added to make them look like paws.

You will need

For an outfit to fit ages 6-9 (finished length of suit about 95cm)

2m of 146cm-wide tiger-printed fur fabric
50cm of 90cm-wide brown felt
40cm strong metal zip
50cm of 1cm-wide elastic
Matching sewing threads
Fabric adhesive
6cm of touch-and-close fastening
Small quantity of wadding for tail
Dressmaker's graph paper

Make-up

Yellow foundation cream
Light-coloured face powder
Black kohl pencil

Preparing the pattern

Using dressmaker's pattern paper, scale up the pattern pieces given on page 62. Mark in all notches, dots, and lines. 1.5cm seams are allowed throughout, and 2.5cm hems on sleeves and trousers.

Cutting out

Open out the fur fabric to full width and place it fur side down. Making sure that pile will run downwards from neck to ankle on all pieces, pin pattern pieces in place as shown in the layout on page 63. As these are cut from single fabric, it is necessary to turn over most of the pattern pieces to obtain the second half (see dotted lines). Using chalk or pencil, mark around the edge of each pattern piece, reversing as necessary, then cut out – using just the tips of the shears to avoid cutting the pile.

For the facings, hood and ear linings, and the boot soles, pin the appropriate pattern pieces to a single layer of felt, as shown in the cutting layout, and cut out.

Transfer all notches, dots, and darts, onto fabric pieces.

Sewing instructions
1 Body
This is stitched with right sides together throughout. Note that seams on fur fabric should be finger-pressed only. Join centre

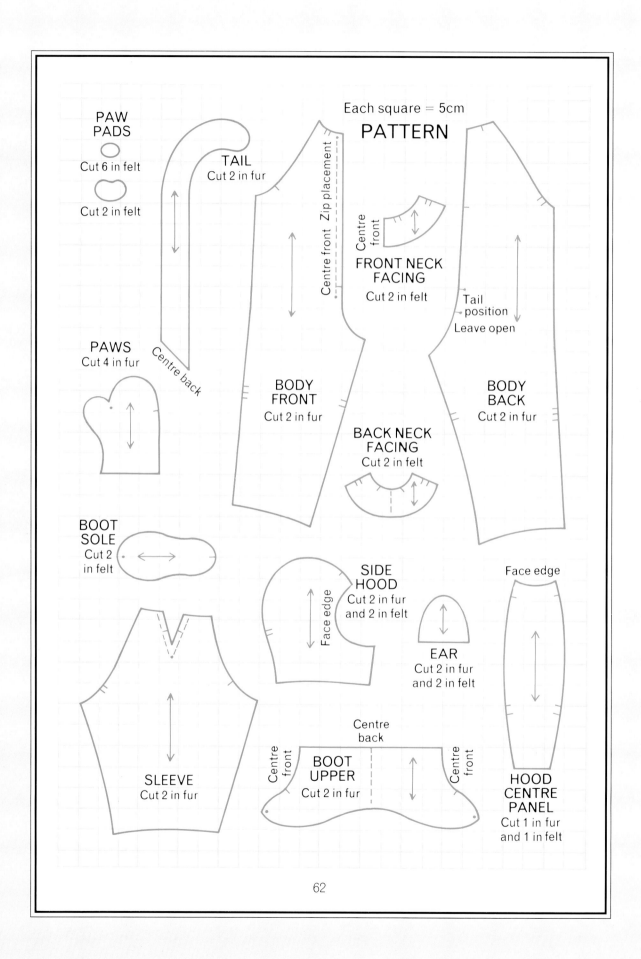

PAW PADS

Cut 6 in felt

Cut 2 in felt

TAIL
Cut 2 in fur

Each square = 5cm
PATTERN

Centre front Zip placement

Centre front

FRONT NECK
FACING
Cut 2 in felt

Tail position
Leave open

PAWS
Cut 4 in fur

Centre back

BODY
FRONT
Cut 2 in fur

BODY
BACK
Cut 2 in fur

BACK NECK
FACING
Cut 2 in felt

BOOT
SOLE
Cut 2
in felt

SIDE
HOOD
Cut 2 in fur
and 2 in felt

Face edge

Face edge

EAR
Cut 2 in fur
and 2 in felt

SLEEVE
Cut 2 in fur

Centre
back

Centre
front

BOOT
UPPER
Cut 2 in fur

Centre
front

HOOD
CENTRE
PANEL
Cut 1 in fur
and 1 in felt

towards the crotch, leaving the upper part open for the zip. Clip into curves.

On the sleeves, stitch shoulder darts to dots and finger-press them open. Matching notches, stitch sleeves to front and back armhole edges, and clip into curves (see illustration opposite).

Tack the zip into the opening placing the slider 2cm from neck edge. Using zipper foot and keeping fur pile clear of the teeth, machine stitch in place.

Matching notches, join front to back at sides, stitching from wrist to ankle, and then join inner leg seam. Clip into curves, and press open.

Turn 2.5cm single hems to wrong side around sleeves and legs, and stick in place.

Matching notches, join shoulder seams of neck facing pieces. Press open. Place the facing onto right side of neckline, with raw edges level and notches matching, and stitch around. Clip seam and turn facing to inside. Slip-stitch front edges of facing to zip tape, and catch-stitch remaining edge to wrong side of fur fabric picking up a single thread only so that the stitches do not show on the right side.

2 Hood

This is stitched with right sides together. On centre panel, machine stitch the side edges

back seam, leaving an opening for the tail between the dots shown on the pattern. Stitch the centre front seam from the dot

Cutting layouts

2m of 146cm fur fabric

50cm of 90cm brown felt

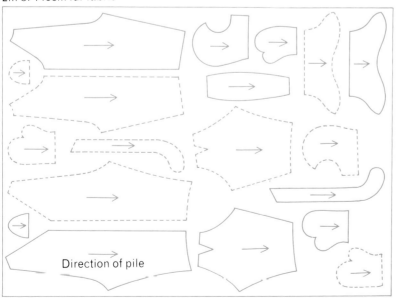

Direction of pile

along the seamline. Clip the fabric up to the stitching. Matching notches, stitch the two main hood pieces to the centre panel, trim and clip the seams. Make up the felt lining in the same way, but leaving a 10cm gap in the stitching of one side panel, near the neck edge, for turning through.

Place the lining inside the hood, and with seams matching, stitch together all round the outer edge. Trim seams and corners and turn through to right side. Slip-stitch

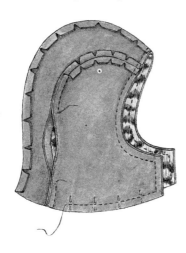

opening closed. Sew small pieces of touch-and-close fastener to inside and outside of front edges, to wrap and fasten hood neatly under the chin.

3 Ears
With right sides together, stitch fur and felt ear pieces around curved edges only. Trim seam and turn through to right side. Fold each ear in half at base, with the felt fabric inside, and hand-stitch firmly to seam of hood, 10cm in from face edge.

4 Boots
With right sides together, and matching notches, stitch centre front seams. Making a 2cm turning, fold upper edge to wrong side and stitch close to raw edge, leaving a small gap in the stitching. Cut two pieces of elastic to fit ankle plus 2.5cm and insert through hem casing. Draw up, overlap ends and stitch firmly. Slip-stitch opening closed.

Matching notches and dots, stitch sole to upper. Trim seam and turn through to right side. Repeat for other boot.

5 Mitts
For the pads, stitch three small and one large oval of felt to fur side of two mitt pieces

placing them as shown in the illustration above. Matching notches, and with right sides together, stitch to corresponding halves of mitt, around curved edge only. Clip seams to dots and trim turnings. Turn under lower edge for 2cm and glue hems in place. Turn through to right side.

Face make-up
1 Apply the yellow cream using a damp sponge to spread it evenly over the entire face. Take it up to the hairline and well below the jawline.

2 To set the foundation make-up, pat it all over lightly with any pale-coloured face powder, and brush away the surplus with a soft make-up brush.

3 Using a sharpened black kohl pencil, and starting with the forehead, draw in a series of curved lines, radiating them outwards from the centre. Continue working down the face, drawing lines over the nose, cheeks and sides of the mouth, thickening the strokes as you work outwards to give a greater realistic effect of tiger stripes. Fill in with shorter lines, where needed.

4 Blacken the oblong nose shape with kohl, then paint in the mouth outline and add the chin markings, again using the black kohl pencil.

Big Fat Hen

This outsize chicken costume will provide endless fun for a child with a sense of humour. The fluffy wings and body are cut from downy fur fabric, and bright red felt is used for the beak and wattle. The ludicrous, gigantic feet are cleverly attached to ankle bootees, to make walking possible.

You will need
For an outfit to fit ages 6-9

3m of 146cm-wide white fur toy fabric
46cm by 46cm square of red felt
1m of 90cm-wide orange felt
Scrap of black felt
Matching sewing threads
45cm by 50cm of heavy weight bonded
    interfacing
2.50m of 2.5cm-wide white bias binding
1m of 1.3cm-wide orange bias binding
1m of 2cm-wide elastic
1m of 1cm-wide elastic
Small quantity of light-weight wadding
1.30m of No. 4 piping cord
Four hooks and eyes
Fabric adhesive
Dressmaker's pattern paper

Make-up
White foundation cream
Orange eye shadow

Accessories
Orange tights or knee socks

Preparing the pattern
Using dressmaker's pattern paper, scale up the pattern pieces given on page 68.

Transfer all notches, dots and lines. Mark in the dart on the hood. 1.5cm seams are allowed throughout, unless otherwise stated. There are no hem allowances, and the pointed and scalloped edges are cut and the raw edges left unfinished. If your fabric frays, use pinking shears for cutting out.

Cutting out
For the body, wings and hood, fold the fur fabric in half, right sides together, with selvedges together at one side and the pile running downwards. Following the cutting layout, place the pattern pieces as shown, and cut out, noting that the body piece is cut out twice to obtain four sections, and centre line of wing placed on a fold.

For the webbed feet and bootees, first cut off 40cm across the 90cm width of orange felt. Fold this piece in half with selvedges meeting at one side. Insert the piece of heavy-weight interfacing between the two layers of felt, then pin one webbed foot pattern in position as shown in the layout. (These will be cut out later.) Open the remaining piece of orange felt and cut out bootee and beak pieces as on layout.

For the coxcomb and wattle, fold the square of red felt in half and pin the pattern pieces in place as shown in the layout. These too will be cut out later.

Transfer notches, dots and dart positions onto all pieces of fur fabric and felt.

Sewing instructions
1 Body
This is stitched with right sides together throughout. Matching double notches, join two body pieces to make the front, and two to make the back. Clip the seam allowances, but do not press. Join front to back at side seams, leaving openings for armholes between the single notches. Catch-stitch or glue turnings of the openings down to wrong side of fabric.

66

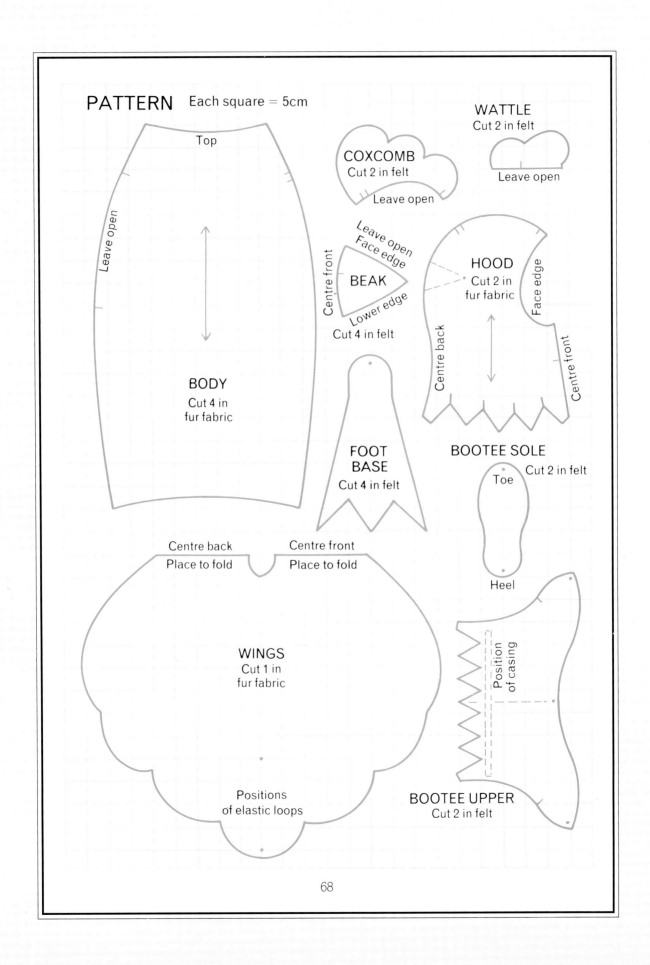

PATTERN   Each square = 5cm

WATTLE
Cut 2 in felt

Leave open

COXCOMB
Cut 2 in felt

Leave open

Top

Leave open

Leave open
Face edge

BEAK

Centre front

Lower edge

Cut 4 in felt

HOOD
Cut 2 in
fur fabric

Face edge

Centre back

Centre front

BODY

Cut 4 in
fur fabric

FOOT
BASE

Cut 4 in felt

BOOTEE SOLE

Cut 2 in felt

Toe

Heel

Centre back
Place to fold

Centre front
Place to fold

Position
of casing

WINGS

Cut 1 in
fur fabric

Positions
of elastic loops

BOOTEE UPPER
Cut 2 in felt

68

Starting and finishing at a centre seam, and leaving 1cm at ends to turn under, stitch the 2.5cm-wide bias binding to the right side of the top and bottom edges. Turn over full width of binding to the inside and stitch in place, close to the lower edge. Into the top casing, insert the cord and knot the ends. This will be drawn up around the neck to fit closely, when worn. Cut a length of 2cm-wide elastic to fit around the child, just below the seat, plus 2.5cm for joining. Insert elastic through lower casing, and stitch to secure. Slipstitch the opening closed.

2 Wings

Open the wing fabric out flat and cut it open along the centre back fold from lower edge to neck. Machine stitch around the neckline, 1.5cm from the raw edge. Clip the turnings up to the stitching line, turn them over to the wrong side and stick down. Sew four evenly spaced hooks and eyes to fasten centre back edges (A)

To form loops for wrists, (B) on inside of wings, attach two pieces of 1cm-wide elastic, each about 25cm long by forming them into a ring and stitching in place, matching the joined ends to the inner dots as shown on the pattern. Cut two further pieces each about 12cm long and attach in the same way, matching the joins to the outer dots. These will form loops to go over the fingers.

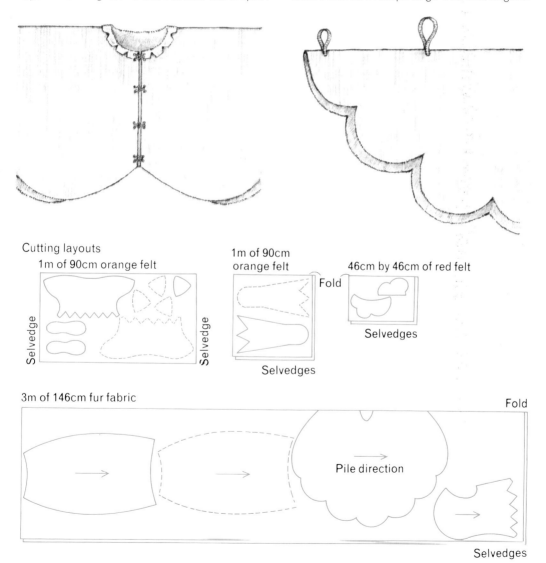

Cutting layouts

1m of 90cm orange felt

Selvedge

Selvedge

1m of 90cm orange felt

Fold

Selvedges

46cm by 46cm of red felt

Selvedges

3m of 146cm fur fabric

Fold

Pile direction

Selvedges

3 Hood

To make the coxcomb and wattle, machine round the pattern shapes that are already pinned to the doubled red felt, leaving the inner edges un-stitched (as marked on pattern). Using pinking shears, cut out close to the stitching. Cut out both the shapes again in wadding, insert into the felt shapes, then close the openings and machine stitch along the seamlines, leaving the pinked edges as decoration. Clip up to the stitching on the inner curve of the coxcomb so that it will fit the curve of the hood and stand up with a more realistic effect.

Fold and stitch the darts of the hood pieces. Cut through the centre of the darts and finger-press the turnings open. Matching notches, and with all raw edges level, tack the coxcomb and wattle to the right side of one hood piece as shown, so that the padded parts lie inwards. Place the second

hood piece on top, pin, tack and stitch the centre front and centre back seams, sandwiching the edges of the coxcomb and wattle between the layers. Remove all the tacking threads.

Machine a line of stitching around the face edge of the hood with a fairly loose tension, 1.5cm in from the raw edge. Clip to the stitching line and turn the clipped edges over to the wrong side. Using fabric adhesive, stick them down to neaten.

4 Beak (optional)

Taking 6mm seams and matching notches, join the beak pieces together along centre front edges to make a pair. Press seams open. Stitch together around lower edge and turn through to the right side.

Cut two layers of wadding a little smaller than finished beak shape and slip inside. Machine the opening closed, 1.5cm in from raw edge. From black felt, cut out two pieces for nostrils, as in the picture, and stick them in place on either side of centre seam. Using one or two overcasting stitches, attach to the inside edges of the hood.

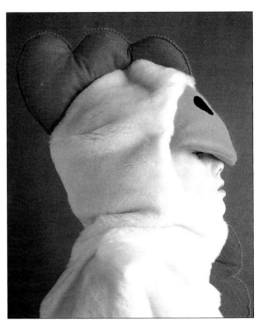

5 Feet

To make the webbed foot base, machine around, close to edge of pattern that is already pinned to doubled felt with interfacing between the layers. Remove pattern and cut out shape, close to the stitching. Stitch and cut out the second foot base in the same way.

For the bootees, make a casing by stitching 1.3cm-wide bias binding across each boot piece at positions marked on the pattern. If desired, pink the pointed edges around tops of bootees. Fold in half right sides together and notches matching, stitch centre front seam, taking 6mm turnings. Insert elastic through casing, draw up to fit ankles, overlap ends and stitch to secure. Matching dots at toes and heels, insert and stitch soles to uppers, taking 6mm seams. Turn through to right side. With heel positions matching, glue or stitch bootees firmly to bases.

Face make-up

1 Apply the white foundation cream over the entire face, using a damp sponge to spread it evenly and to give a smooth, matt finish. Take it up to the hairline, and below the jawline.

2 Using a soft applicator, colour the eyelids with orange eye shadow.

3 Should you prefer the chicken without the felt beak, simply colour the nose with orange eye shadow to give the impression of a beak.

Funny Bunny

Just the thing for the easter parade this giant rabbit wears a costume made from glossy fur fabric, combined with felt details. In his mittened paws he clutches an enormous felt carrot, for an extra touch of fun.

You will need
For an outfit to fit ages 6-9

2m of 146cm-wide fur fabric
50cm of 90cm-wide beige felt
1m of 90cm-wide orange felt
30cm of 90cm-wide bright green felt
Matching sewing threads
Toy filling (or cut-up fabric scraps)
40cm strong metal zip
6cm of touch-and-close fastener
50cm of 1cm-wide elastic
Ball of knitting yarn in white or beige
Small pieces of card
Fabric adhesive
Dressmaker's pattern paper

Make-up
Peach-coloured foundation cream
Face powder in peach, bright pink, and light
  brown
Eye pencils in white and pink
Brown kohl pencil

Preparing the pattern
Scale up the pattern pieces given on page 62 for the tiger outfit, omitting the ears and tail. Substitute the rabbit's ears and add the carrot pattern, by following the diagrams on page 74.

Cutting out
Follow the instructions for cutting out the tiger costume, but substitute the layouts for the rabbit outfit.
  For the carrot top, cut out two oblong pieces from the green felt, each one measuring 35cm by 25cm.

Sewing Instructions
1 Body
Make up in the same way as for the tiger (see page 63) but stitch the entire back seam, without leaving a gap for the tail. (The rabbit's tail will be sewn on to the outside, at the same position.)

2 Hood
Follow the instructions for the tiger's hood.

3 Ears
Place fur and fabric pieces with right sides together and stitch long sides to top point.

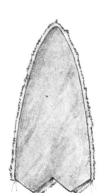

Trim point and turn through to right side. Pleat the lower edge of each ear, through both thicknesses, and stitch to side seams of hood, about 12cm in from face edge.

4 Mitts
Make up as for the tiger's mitts.

PATTERN

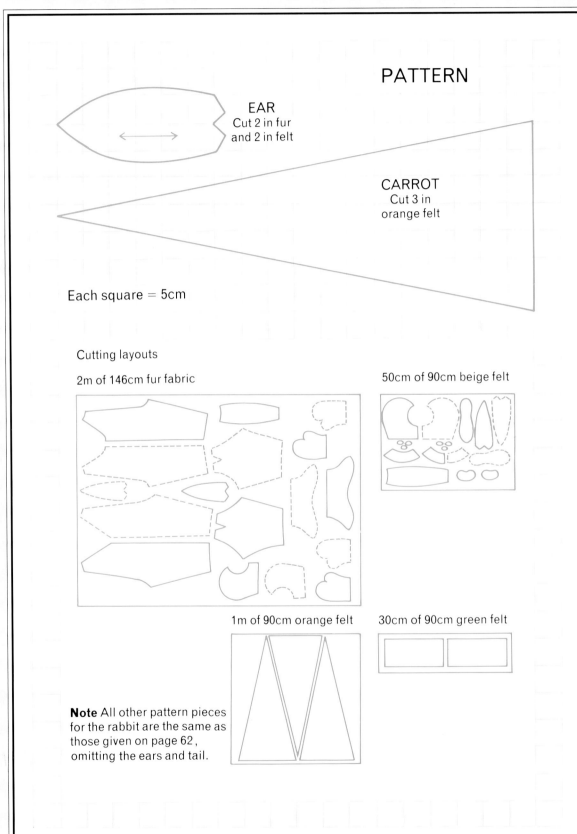

EAR
Cut 2 in fur
and 2 in felt

CARROT
Cut 3 in
orange felt

Each square = 5cm

Cutting layouts

2m of 146cm fur fabric

50cm of 90cm beige felt

1m of 90cm orange felt

30cm of 90cm green felt

Note All other pattern pieces
for the rabbit are the same as
those given on page 62,
omitting the ears and tail.

5 Boots
Make up as for the tiger.

6 Tail
Make a pompon from knitting yarn: cut out two circles in card each with the diameter of the required size pompon (about 12cm). Cut holes about 2p piece size in the centre of each one. Wind off some lengths of knitting yarn into tiny hanks, and wrap the yarn around the double discs, passing it through the centre hole. Continue until the hole is almost closed, then cut through the loops of yarn at the outer edge. Carefully prise the card discs slightly apart, and with a spare piece of yarn, tie the strands together tightly and firmly, leaving one long end for threading. Remove card and fluff into a ball. Using free end of yarn, stitch pompon to back of suit at tail position.

7 Carrot
Taking 6mm seams, (with points meeting, and raw edges level) and with right sides together, stitch the long edges of the three carrot pieces together. Round off the point when stitching the third seam. Turn through to right side and stuff firmly. Gather around top edge, draw it up tightly and fasten off the thread securely.

Using pinking shears, make vertical cuts down one long edge of each green rectangle. Roll one up tightly to form the centre of the carrot top and stick down the end (see illustration opposite). Stitch this in place at the base, placing it into the hole at the centre of the carrot. Gather along the un-cut edge of the second green felt piece, draw it up and stitch it in place, to surround the top of the carrot.

Face make-up
1 Apply the peach-coloured foundation cream over the entire face fading it out towards the hair and jawline.

2 Pat on peach face powder, and brush away the surplus with a soft make-up brush.

3 Using a very soft pink eye pencil draw in the outline of the eye, in an exaggerated, upturned shape, then fill in the area with white eye pencil. Outline the white shape with brown kohl. Sketch in the mouth shape, in the same way as for the eyes, filling inside the line with white, then outline with the brown kohl.

4 Using a brush and brown powder, shade in the sides of the nose, and the cheeks.

5 Dot in appropriate whiskers, and draw fine, upward-curving lines around the mouth, with brown kohl pencil.

6 Colour the nose with pink powder. Then draw a few lines around the outline of the mouth to give the effect of fur.

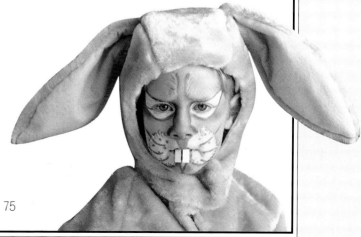

Stitch a Witch

This spooky witch costume would be ideal for a Hallowe'en party. A tattered dress is crowned with the traditional pointed hat and to complete this picture of blackest magic there is a wicked-looking snake with pink eyes. He is wired inside so that he can be formed into realistic coils, and his markings are picked out in shiny pink sequins.

You will need
For an outfit to fit ages 6-9 (dress length about 104cm from the shoulder)

2m of 115cm-wide black polyester/cotton
50cm of 115cm-wide black polyester/cotton for
    separate collar (optional)
Two black press studs
Black bias binding
Matching sewing threads
1m of 90cm-wide black felt
50cm by 50cm of upholstery buckram
48cm by 58cm sheet of cartridge or other
    stiff paper
Two skeins of scarlet raffia
Fabric adhesive
Dressmaker's pattern paper
2m of milliner's wire
Pair of toy animal's eyes in pink – or two
    small pink buttons
1m by 20cm strip of green lurex jersey
Scrap of red felt for snake's tongue
60cm-long strip of pink sequin trim
Small quantity of synthetic wadding, or
    cushion filling

Make-up
Mint-green pan stick
Eye shadow in brown, light and dark green
Black lipstick
Black kohl pencil

Accessories
Black tights
Black shoes
Broomstick

Preparing the pattern
Using dressmaker's pattern paper, scale up the pattern pieces given on page 78. Use the same dress pattern piece for both back and front, cutting the neckline as instructed. Cut the pattern on the solid line for the back neckline, and for the front neckline cut along the dashed line. Seam allowances of 1.5cm are included; there are no hems on sleeves or skirt which are left with raw edges. For the hat brim, cut out the pattern along the solid line of the inner and outer circles. Transfer notches and other marks onto each pattern piece. Make a pattern for the separate collar, if desired.

Cutting out
For the dress and collar, fold the fabrics with selvedges together along one side, pin the pattern pieces in position as shown in the cutting layouts, and cut out.
    For the hat, first cut out the crown section in stiff paper. Open the felt to the full width and cut out the crown and one brim piece, to the solid line. Trim 1cm away, all round the inner and outer circle of the brim pattern and cut the second brim piece in felt, as shown in the cutting layout. Now, using the trimmed pattern, cut a second brim piece in upholstery buckram, for stiffening.

Sewing instructions
1 Dress
This is stitched with right sides together throughout. Join front to back at shoulders, stitching from wrist to neck edge. Press

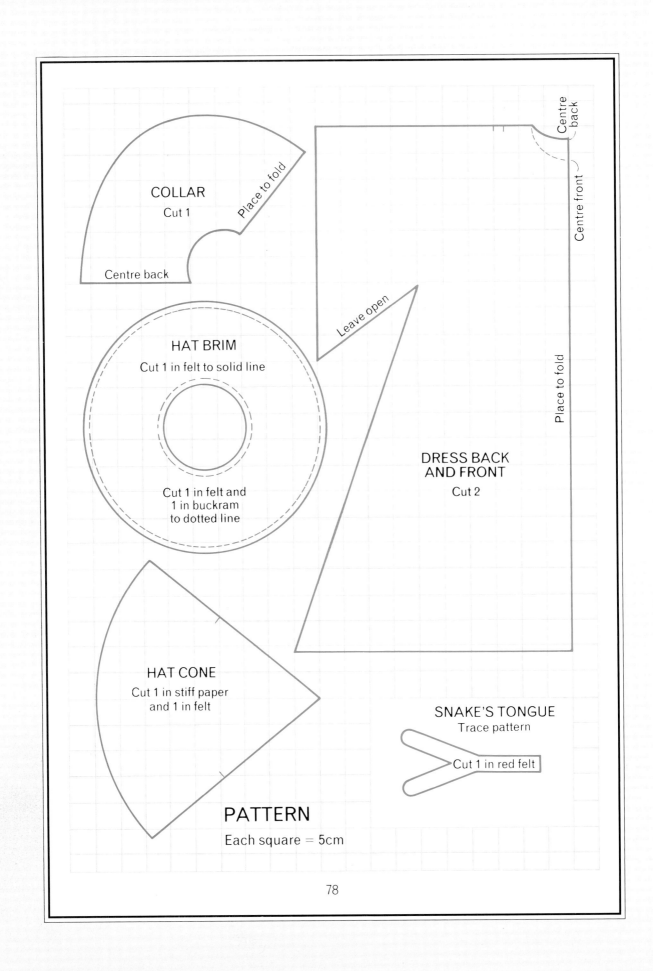

COLLAR
Cut 1

Place to fold

Centre back

Centre back

Centre front

HAT BRIM

Cut 1 in felt to solid line

Cut 1 in felt and
1 in buckram
to dotted line

Leave open

Place to fold

DRESS BACK
AND FRONT

Cut 2

HAT CONE

Cut 1 in stiff paper
and 1 in felt

SNAKE'S TONGUE
Trace pattern

Cut 1 in red felt

PATTERN

Each square = 5cm

seams open. For the neck opening, cut a 15cm slit down the centre back. Using black bias binding, bind the raw edge of the neckline and opening in one operation, starting and finishing at the centre back.

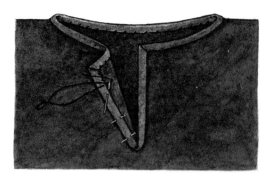

Join back to front at side seams stitching up to point of underarm only, leaving under-sleeve seams open. Press seams open and clip seam at underarm. Sew on a press stud to fasten neckline opening.

Using the four left-over strips of fabric, attach the pointed ends of each pair to either side of the neckline, on the shoulder seam, leaving ends free. Use opened scissors to 'tear' partway through these fabric strips to make tatters. Cut or tear the lower edges of the sleeves and skirt in a similar way.

For the separate collar, open out and make narrow hems along straight edges. Bind the neckline with bias binding and sew a press stud to the neck edge to fasten at the centre back. Cut the lower edge into tatters, as for the dress.

2 Snake

Bend the length of milliner's wire in half. Twist the loop end to form a head, about 12cm long. Twist the remaining wire together along the length, to form the body.

Place the strip of lurex fabric right side down on the table. Spread a layer of wadding evenly over the fabric, place the wire frame on top and then cover with more wadding. Bring the edges of the fabric together, fold them in, one over the other and slip-stitch them in place, moulding the snake shape as you go.

Cut away the shanks from toy animal eyes and stick one on each side of the snake's head, (or sew on buttons for eyes, if preferred).

Decorate the head and along the back of the snake with the sequin trim, as in the picture, stitching or sticking it in place to form a broad zigzag pattern along its back. Using the trace pattern, cut out the forked tongue from the red felt, and stitch the short straight end in position.

Cutting layouts
1m of 90cm black felt (single layer)

Selvedge

2m of 115cm black fabric

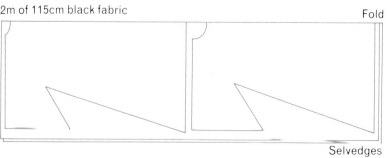

50cm of 115cm black fabric

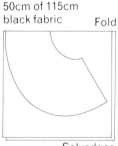

3 Hat
Using fabric adhesive, stick the stiff paper to the felt crown piece. Shape it into a cone, overlap the straight edges and stick them in position. Hold with a paper clip until dry.

Place the buckram brim piece centrally onto the larger felt brim, so that the 1cm turnings extend evenly around the edges of the inner and outer circles. Clip into the turnings, close to the buckram as shown in the diagram below. Dampen the extreme edges of the buckram, on both circles, and with a warm iron, press the turnings onto it.

Place the stiffened brim over the cone, with buckram underneath, and pull it down close to base of cone. Clip around base of crown for 1.5cm and stick the turning on to underside of brim. When dry, stick the second brim piece evenly in place, on to the stiffened brim, covering the turnings.

4 Hair
For the hair, cut the raffia into varying lengths and divide into two bunches. With one end of each bunch level, machine raffia to 5cm-long strips of binding. Stick ends of binding to inside of crown, one on each side. Or, simply hold with adhesive tape.

Face make-up (wicked witch)
1 Using mint-green pan stick, smooth over the entire face from the hairline to the jawline, and set with plenty of loose powder.

2 Using a thick brush and dark green eye shadow, shade in the temples, jawline, forehead, under the eyes and the sides of the nose, from the nostrils to the corners of the mouth.

3 Apply paler green colours as highlights to the chin, nose and cheekbones, blending them well in.

4 Suggest wrinkles by blending in brown shades, following the areas where they would naturally appear.

5 Paint the lips black. Then draw in the arched eyebrows with soft kohl pencil taking them above the natural line.

For a 'good' witch (see page 77) simply apply yellow foundation cream to the entire face, and darken the eyebrows with kohl.

Space Invader

A glittering, neon-bright collection of lamé fabrics adorns this visitor from another planet. Her space gun and hat decoration are made from stiff card and her curious headdress is formed over a buckram base. Wadding is skilfully used to pad out the alien shape of her tunic, leg and arm bands.

You will need
For an outfit to fit ages 6-9 (length of tunic is about 58cm)

1.50m of 115cm-wide transfer lamé in silver
50cm each of four different brightly-coloured transfer lamé fabrics
Matching sewing threads
1m of lightweight wadding
Bag of toy stuffing or cushion filling
70cm of 90cm-wide heavy bonded interfacing
50cm of heavy iron-on interfacing
Buckle for 3.5cm-wide belt
Small piece of stout card for space gun
54cm of touch-and-close fastening
30cm by 24cm piece of grey felt
Buckram cap shape
Fabric adhesive
Dressmaker's pattern paper

Make-up
White foundation cream
Face powder in white and gold
Eye liner pencils and eye shadow in purple, blue, pink and gold
Black mascara

Accessories
White long-sleeved polo neck sweater
White tights

Preparing the pattern
Using dressmaker's pattern paper, scale up the pattern pieces given on page 84. The leg and arm band pieces can be marked out directly onto bonded sew-in interfacing. Pattern pieces are not given for the coloured 'tubes' which are made from straight strips of fabric and stuffed with filling.

1.5cm turnings have been allowed on all seams. There is no hem at lower edge of the tunic as non-fraying fabric has been used. Mark notches, dots, and lines, onto pattern.

Cutting out
Fold the silver fabric in half lengthwise with selvedges together at one side, and pin pattern pieces in place as shown in the cutting layout. Cut out, remembering to place the half-shoe pattern to a fold, and to cut a strip for the belt from a single layer.

From the grey felt, cut out two soles, for the shoes. From wadding, cut out front and back yoke pieces, and cut these pieces again in the iron-on interfacing. From the heavy sew-in interfacing, cut out the leg and arm band pieces (following diagram 3 page 86–7) plus a strip for stiffening belt, 3cm wide by waist measurement plus 25cm.

From each of the four coloured lamé fabrics, cut one back panel for the hat, as shown on the pattern. The remainder of the coloured fabric will be used for the tubes and trims on the hat and space gun. Transfer all pattern markings onto fabrics.

Sewing instructions
1 Tunic
This is stitched with right sides together throughout. Press iron-on interfacing to wrong sides of lamé yoke pieces. Place the wadding yoke pieces on top of this and tack together around the edge. Machine wadding to fabric around lower edge and trim

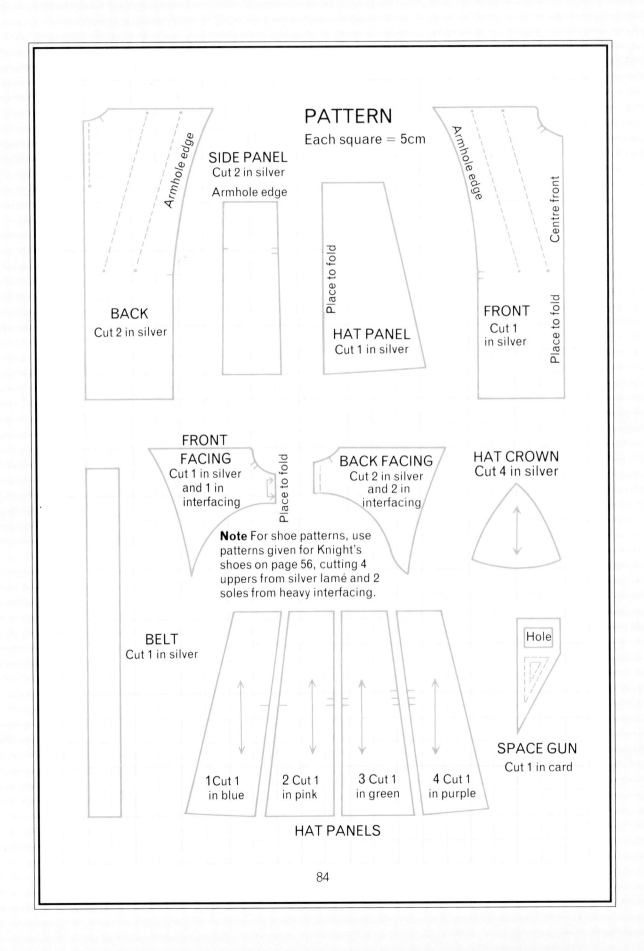

PATTERN
Each square = 5cm

SIDE PANEL
Cut 2 in silver

Armhole edge

BACK
Cut 2 in silver

Armhole edge

Place to fold

HAT PANEL
Cut 1 in silver

Armhole edge

Centre front

Place to fold

FRONT
Cut 1
in silver

FRONT FACING
Cut 1 in silver
and 1 in
interfacing

Place to fold

BACK FACING
Cut 2 in silver
and 2 in
interfacing

HAT CROWN
Cut 4 in silver

Note For shoe patterns, use
patterns given for Knight's
shoes on page 56, cutting 4
uppers from silver lamé and 2
soles from heavy interfacing.

BELT
Cut 1 in silver

Hole

SPACE GUN
Cut 1 in card

1 Cut 1
in blue

2 Cut 1
in pink

3 Cut 1
in green

4 Cut 1
in purple

HAT PANELS

excess turnings below stitching line. Matching notches, stitch facings to neck and armhole edges of front and back tunic. Trim and clip seam. Turn facings inside.

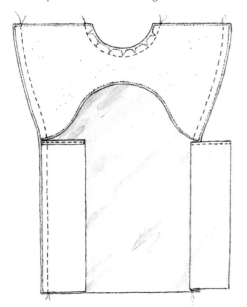

On one side panel, turn under 1.5cm to wrong side across top (armhole) edge and top-stitch. Repeat for other side panel. Matching notches, stitch side panels to front and back pieces. Join front to back at shoulders, stitching through all layers. Press seams open. Trim and top-stitch shoulder seams flat, on either side of seam. Top-stitch along armholes and continue down side seams at front and back.

Turn under facing at centre back for 1.5cm, top-stitch round neckline, catching in facing. Join centre back seam from lower edge to dot. Press open. Stitch touch-and-close fastener along back neck opening, one half projecting from edge, to fasten neck.

To make the coloured tube trims, cut (across the width) one strip from each of the four coloured fabrics, each measuring 74cm by 10cm. Fold each strip in half lengthwise and stitch along long edge. Turn them through and stuff firmly to within about 5mm of ends. With seams at centre back of each tube, turn short ends under and top-stitch. Stick, underside of each tube to front/back of tunic over shoulder, following dashed lines shown on pattern.

2 Belt
Cut belt piece to waist length plus 25cm for overlap. Cut a 3.5cm-wide strip of wadding to belt length, place it centrally on to wrong side of fabric strip. Lay the belt stiffening on top and tack together. Fold turnings of silver fabric over onto interfacing and stitch along long sides and one short end, about 6mm in from folded edge. Attach buckle securely to unstitched end.

3 Shoes
Open out lamé shoe pieces and tack wadding to wrong side. Right sides together, and matching dots, join centre front seams. Quilt, following dashed lines on pattern.

Cutting layout
1.70m of 115cm silver lamé

Fold

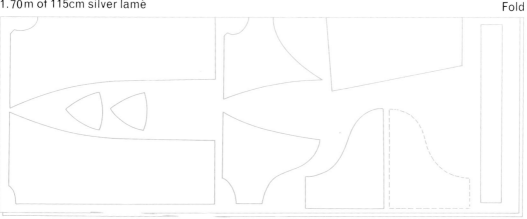

Selvedges

With shoes right side out, insert inner soles and stick the turnings at lower edges of shoes down onto underside of soles, clipping turnings. Stick the felt soles on the outside, to neaten. Apply adhesive to the shoe stiffeners and push one into the heel and toe of each shoe. Pad the toes with wadding.

4 Gun
Cut pattern from card and cut out centre. Spray with metallic silver paint, or cover it with scraps of the silver lamé. Trim with triangles of card, covered with the coloured fabrics glued in place.

5 Hat
With right sides together, join four hat segments to fit buckram form. Press seams open and place over buckram shape. Pull down tightly, turn under the lower edge for 1.5cm and stitch or stick fabric to buckram.

Make the back flap by joining the coloured panels 1-4 with right sides together and matching notches. Press the seams open.

Join the striped panel with right sides together to the silver panel along straight sides and lower edge. Trim seam and corners, and turn through to right side. Press edges. With the striped side nearest to the head, stitch top edge of panel to inside edge of hat shape. To trim, cover triangular pieces of card with coloured fabric and stick them to front of hat.

6 Leg bands
(For each band) cut four strips of lamé, one in each of the colours, measuring 33cm by 11cm. Mark lines onto interfacing, as shown in diagram A (above). Place first strip right

Diagram A
LEG BAND BACKING
Cut 2 in heavy interfacing

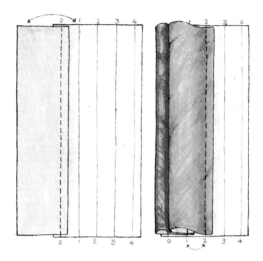

side down onto marked side of interfacing. Overlap the inner edge so that the seamline of strip will be exactly over the first dashed line on the interfacing. Stitch along this line. Now bring other long edge of the same strip over onto line 1 right side up, and machine it in place along seamline, thus forming a tube of fabric. Place the second colour strip, with right sides facing and raw edges of strips together, to line 1 and machine stitch. Turn this strip over to right side and stitch the edge, on seamline, down to line 2. Repeat with other strips, to make four, open tubes on the surface of the interfacing. Stuff tubes firmly to within 5mm of ends. Machine across ends to enclose the filling. Cut two strips of silver fabric, each 12.5cm

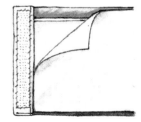

by 7cm, turn seam allowances under all round and enclose raw ends of band inside

86

folded strips. Stitch through all layers. To neaten back cut a rectangle of silver fabric to size, turn under interfacing at sides, and stick fabric in place. Attach touch-and-close fastener to inside and outside short ends of band to wrap and fasten when worn. Repeat for second leg band.

7 Arm bands
Following diagram B (see below), mark out interfacing rectangles. Cut strips of coloured lamé 11cm wide by 27cm long and make up as for the leg bands.

Diagram B
ARM BAND BACKING
Cut 2 in heavy interfacing

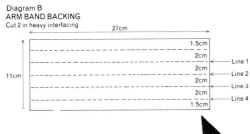

Face make-up
1 Apply white foundation cream over the entire face. Use a damp sponge to spread it evenly, taking it up to the hairline and down below the jawline.

2 Set the make-up by patting on white face powder, and brushing away the surplus with a soft make-up brush.

3 Using eyeliner pencils in purple and pink, draw in zigzag lines diagonally across the face, filling them in with solid colour.

4 Using soft applicators and eye shadows, make up the eyes with purple, blue, gold and pink, sweeping them outwards on the eyelids. Blend in each colour carefully, as you go.

5 Darken the lashes with black mascara, and pat gold powder onto the lips.

Out for the Count

This outfit shows Count Dracula at his most frighteningly elegant. He sports a swirly black cape lined with vivid scarlet satin, worn over black trousers and a smart dicky made from white piqué, plus a large black bow-tie. Add appropriately sinister make-up, and he is ready for anything!

You will need

For an outfit to fit ages 6-9 (trouser length, 82cm, cloak length about 78cm)

3.70m of 115cm-wide black satin
2m of 115cm-wide scarlet satin
50cm of 90cm-wide white piqué
20cm by 45cm of medium-weight sew-in bonded interfacing
Matching sewing threads
70cm of 1cm-wide elastic
1.50m of fine red cord
2cm of touch-and-close fastener
Dressmaker's pattern paper

Make-up

White foundation cream
Black kohl pencil
Eye shadow in red and grey
Lipstick in red and black

Accessories

Black shiny shoes
Black socks
Joke fangs
White gloves
Black silver-topped cane

Preparing the pattern

Using dressmaker's pattern paper, scale up the pattern pieces given on page 90. The bow-tie is made from straight strips of black satin, so a paper pattern is not needed. For the trouser pattern, use the full length version given on page 22. 1.5cm seam allowances are included unless otherwise stated, and 3cm hem allowances on the trousers. The cloak is fully lined to the outer edges, so there are no hems.

Mark in all straight-grain lines, notches, dots and letters A and B on cloak pattern.

Cutting out

Open out the black fabric to its full width and then fold it crossways in half, so that the selvedges meet along both sides, and with the fold along one end.

Place the pattern pieces for the cloak and the trousers onto the fabric, as shown in the cutting layout, making sure the arrow lines follow the straight grain of the fabric. Cut out the cloak pattern piece twice, to obtain four pieces. Cut out the half-collar pattern with a short end to the fold. From the remaining fabric, cut out one rectangle measuring 17cm by 23cm and another, 8cm by 5cm, for the bow-tie and knot.

Open out the red fabric, and re-fold as for the black. Following the lining cutting layout, cut out the cloak pattern twice and the collar piece once, placing it to a fold.

Following the cutting layout for the white fabric, cut out pieces for the dicky front. Cut out the collar piece from double fabric, and the bib from a single layer. From the interfacing, cut out the collar piece once.

Transfer all notches, dots and letters to the appropriate fabric pieces.

Sewing instructions
1 Cloak

This is stitched with right sides together throughout. Join two black cloak pieces

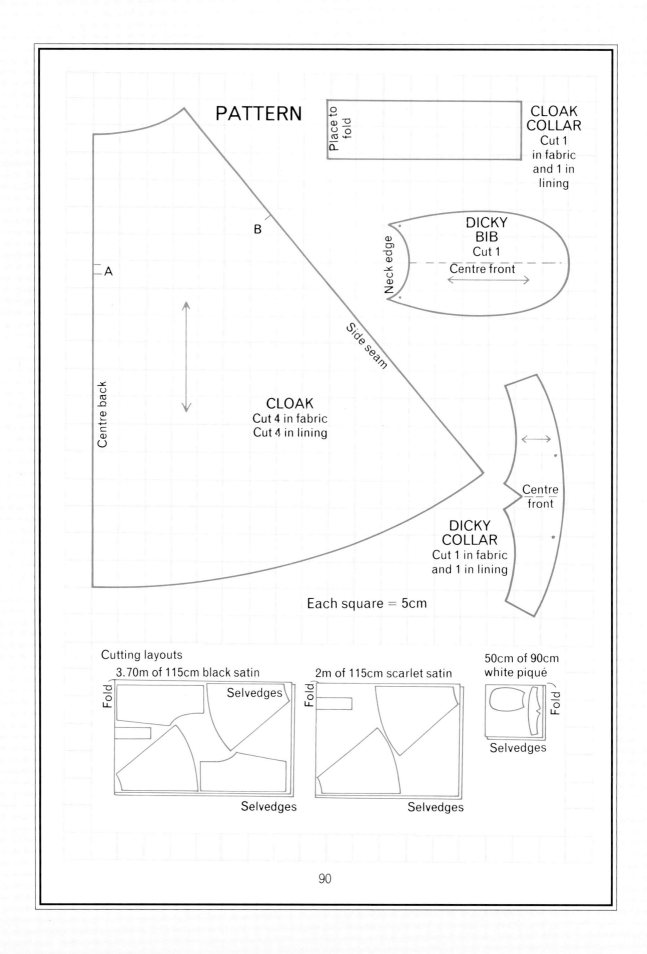

PATTERN

CLOAK COLLAR
Cut 1 in fabric and 1 in lining

Place to fold

DICKY BIB
Cut 1

Neck edge

Centre front

B

A

Side seam

Centre back

CLOAK
Cut 4 in fabric
Cut 4 in lining

DICKY COLLAR
Cut 1 in fabric and 1 in lining

Centre front

Each square = 5cm

Cutting layouts

3.70m of 115cm black satin

Fold

Selvedges

Selvedges

2m of 115cm scarlet satin

Fold

Selvedges

50cm of 90cm white piqué

Fold

Selvedges

together along the edge marked A, matching the double notches. Press the seam open: this becomes the centre back seam. Open cloak back out flat, right side up, and matching single notches, join the third and fourth cloak pieces to either side of cloak back, along edges marked B. Press seams open. Repeat for the red lining pieces, making them up in the same way.

Place the red and black cloak layers together, with all raw edges and seamlines matching, and stitch together down straight edges and around curved lower edge, leaving neck edge open. Clip corners, trim seams and turn through to right side. Press. Tack the raw edges of neckline together.

Join the red and black collar pieces together along one long edge. Trim the seam and press both edges towards the lining. Turn under and press 1.5cm across both short ends, and then 1.5cm on the long edge of the lining only. Mark centre point of the long, unpressed edge, and matching this point to the centre back cloak seam, pin and stitch the open collar to neck edge of cloak, through all layers. Trim seam, clip around curve and press seam towards collar. Bring the longer pressed edge of collar lining over neckline seam, and with the fold level with the previous line of stitching, edge-stitch collar lining in place, through all layers.

To form a channel for the cord, machine a second, parallel line of stitching, on the collar, 1.3cm above the edge-stitching. Thread cord through channel, draw up, and tie in a bow to fasten. Trim and knot ends.

2 Dicky and bow-tie

Neaten around longer raw edge of bib piece, (omitting neckline) then turn the neatened edge under for 6mm and edge-stitch by machine. Press thoroughly on the wrong side.

Tack interfacing to wrong side of one collar piece. With right sides together and matching centre notches and side dots, pin and stitch neck edge of bib to centre section of interfaced collar piece. Clip into curve

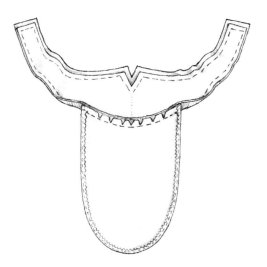

and press seam onto collar. With right sides together, join collar pieces from dot to dot, stitching around upper edge, leaving the central bib area open. Trim corners and seam. Clip to stitching at centre, between collar points, turn through to right side and press. Slip-stitch opening closed. Stitch pieces of touch-and-close fastener to the short ends so that they will wrap over at the back of the neck and hold the collar in place. To form the wings of the collar, turn the points over and press them firmly so that they stand out at right angles to the dicky front just above the bow.

For the bow-tie, fold the larger rectangle of black satin in half along the 23cm length. Stitch across the short ends and the long side, leaving a 5cm gap in the centre. Trim seam and corners and turn through to the right side. Press, then stitch the opening closed. Bring the short ends to meet at the centre back, and stitch them in place through all thicknesses.

For the knot, fold under 1cm on the longer

edges of the smaller rectangle, and press on the wrong side. Wrap the strip around the centre of the bow and catch-stitch the ends together at the back. Using matching thread, stitch the finished bow in place to the centre front of the collar, picking up a small amount of fabric beneath the knot and stitching through all layers.

3 Trousers
These are stitched with right sides together throughout. To prevent satin fabric from slipping, you will find it easier if you pin and tack the seams before machining. With notches matching, join right leg front to right leg back along the inner leg seam; repeat for left leg and press the seams open. Matching the notches, join the side seam of each leg and press them open under a dry pressing cloth. With the wrong sides outside, place one complete trouser leg inside the other and, matching notches and inner leg seams, stitch the crotch seam from back waist to front waist edge (see page 46). Trim the curved seam to 1cm wide, and press open.

To make a channel at the waist edge, press 5mm to the wrong side, then turn over for a further 2.5cm. Insert ribbon loops for hanging up, if preferred. Stitch close to bottom fold, leaving a small gap in the stitching. Cut a length of elastic to fit the waist, plus 2.5cm for turnings. Insert the elastic into the casing, draw it up, and then overlap and sew the ends firmly together. Slip-stitch the opening closed. Make similar hems around the bottoms of the legs, but hand-stitch the pressed edge in place and omit the elastic. Remove all tacking threads. Press under a dry pressing cloth.

Face make-up
1 Apply white foundation cream, using a damp sponge to spread it evenly over the face. Take it up to the hairline and below the jawline.

2 Emphasize the eyebrows by shading them in using a soft black kohl pencil, and curving them upwards towards the outer edges.

3 Using a lipbrush, or small applicator, mark a line with red eye shadow, just under the eyes. Add a little grey eye shadow around the sockets, along the temples and under the cheekbones.

4 Colour the lips with a black lipstick.

5 Using a lip brush and red lipstick, paint in 'blood drops' around the mouth, running down the chin and over the tips of the fangs, for a more frightening effect.

Suppliers

The stockists listed below have a mail order service.
Either telephone first or send a stamped addressed
envelope with your initial enquiry.

**Dress-weight fabrics, interfacings,
felt haberdashery**

John Lewis Partnership
Oxford Street
London W1
01-629 7711

**Novelty fabrics, plain and
printed satins, nets**

Borovick Fabrics Limited
16 Berwick Street
London WN1 4HP
01-437 2180

By The Yard
14 Berwick Street
London W1
01-434 2389

Fur fabrics, felt

Equality fur fabrics
20 London Road
Apsley
Hemel Hempstead
Herts HP3 9SB
(0442) 64854

Beryls
134 Manor Way
Ruislip Manor
Middlesex
(0895) 623698

**Make-up, hats, fangs,
toy pistols, swords**

Giggles (Personal shoppers only)
Bridge House
119–123 Station Road
Hayes
Middlesex
01-848 7372
Also at:
Harrow
01-863 3691
Watford
(0923) 28892

**Theatrical make-up, gold and
silver powders, paints**

Brodie and Middleton
68 Drury Lane
London WC2
01-629 9964

Acknowledgements

The publishers would like to extend special thanks to the
following people for their help in the production of this book:

Models
Mathew Austin
Rachel Austin
Simon Briault
Martyn Clutterbuck
Rebecca Dewing
Nicholas Melville
Rosie Melville

Face Make-up
Ozzie Alam

Photography
John Melville

Illustrators
Sally Holmes
John Hutchinson

93